WHO ME COOK?

by

Mark Feldstein & Gael Fischer

introducing "CHOMP"

as your guide

Illustrations by Gael Fischer & Louis Batongmalaque

©1982 Mark Feldstein & Gael Fischer

ISBN 0-912659-00-9
Printed in the United States of America.
Published by damgood books
10500 National Blvd.
Los Angeles, CA. 90234

WHY NOT ?

You ARE A PRIME CANDIDATE FOR THIS COOKBOOK IF:

1) AFTER WORKING ALL DAY, YOU WISH THAT MOM WAS STILL AROUND TO FIX YOUR MEALS.

2) YOUR IDEA OF COOKING IS SOMETHING BETWEEN DEFROSTING AND HEATING UP.

3) YOU AND THE EMPLOYEES OF THE NEAREST FAST FOOD RESTAURANT ARE ON A FIRST NAME BASIS.

4) YOU'RE TIRED OF COOKBOOKS THAT OFFER 3-HOUR, 20-STEP "QUICK & EASY" RECIPES.

5) YOUR SPOUSE IS INDISPOSED (PREGNANT, OUT OF TOWN, TOO DARN TIRED TO COOK, ETC.) AND YOU NEED TO MEET THE CHALLENGE OF THE KITCHEN OR STARVE.

MOST COOKBOOKS MAKE YOU FEEL BURIED UNDER TOO MANY
RECIPES, INGREDIENTS, AND UNNECESSARY EQUIPMENT.

MOST COOKBOOKS OVERWHELM THE READER WITH TOO MANY RECIPES, MAKING DECISIONS VERY DIFFICULT, AND PLANNING A WEEK OF MEALS NEARLY IMPOSSIBLE.

MOST COOKBOOKS ASSUME THAT THE READER KNOWS MORE THAN HE DOES.

MOST COOKBOOKS EVENTUALLY CALL FOR EXPENSIVE INGREDIENTS OR SIMPLY MORE INGREDIENTS THAN ARE NECESSARY FOR AN ECONOMICAL MEAL.

WHO ME COOK? IS **NOT** "MOST COOKBOOKS." IT'S A METHOD OF ORGANIZATION, PLANNING, AND PERFECT EXECUTION THAT REDUCES WORK TO A MINIMUM.

WE HAVE FOUND THIS KIND OF LIST-MAKING, SCHEDULING, AND PLANNING WORKS BEAUTIFULLY! THE BEST PART IS THAT **WE** HAVE DONE IT FOR YOU.

ALL **YOU** HAVE TO DO IS FOLLOW THE STEP-BY-STEP INSTRUCTIONS AND LEAVE THE PLANNING TO US.

WITH SCHEDULES, SHOPPING LISTS AND RECIPES, DINNERS APPEAR LIKE MAGIC.

HOW DO WE DO THIS FOR YOU?

BY GIVING YOU:

1. BASIC, TASTY, SIMPLE-TO-MAKE RECIPES. YOU'LL NEVER NEED EXPENSIVE INGREDIENTS OR MORE THAN SIX SPICES IN THE HOUSE.

2. WEEKLY DINNER SCHEDULES WITH MENU PLANS TO ORGANIZE YOUR MEALS.

3. WEEKLY SHOPPING LISTS DRAWN FROM THE RECIPES. THESE CAN BE TORN OUT OF THE BOOK AND TAKEN TO THE SUPERMARKET TO MAKE SHOPPING FAST AND ECONOMICAL:

   — CUTS YOUR SHOPPING DOWN TO ONCE A WEEK.
   — NO MORE EXPENSIVE IMPULSE BUYING.
   — NO MORE ENDLESS SUPERMARKET WANDERING IN SEARCH OF MEALS.

ENOUGH EXPLANATIONS . . . LETS START COOKIN'!

TABLE OF CONTENTS

GENERAL HINTS

1. Organize! Take out all necessary ingredients and equipment BEFORE you begin to cook.

2. Be sure your BASIC SHOPPING LIST stock is complete.

3. Don't hesitate to taste while cooking - it is, of course, the ultimate test!

4. Never freeze anything once it has been frozen and defrosted.

5. Don't cook every night. Even though we have scheduled each night of the week, we recommend you take at least one night a week off: being an extremist (even in cooking!) is never a good idea. Visit a friend, fix a sandwich, eat out. Just remember, you will have enough food for 7 dinners with the preplanned shopping lists, so if you skip one night, the days on the schedules can be changed.

6. Remember to check your next day's meal for items that may need defrosting.

7. Save any bottles (especially wide-necked) for storing leftovers.

REQUIRED READING

To benefit the most from WHO ME COOK? read the following pages:

EACH CHAPTER INTRODUCTION:

SCHEDULES and SHOPPING LISTS

SCHEDULES AND SHOPPING LISTS

THE FOLLOWING PAGES ARE YOUR
KEY TO SIMPLIFIED MEAL PLANS AND
SHOPPING. EACH SCHEDULE IS FOLLOWED
BY THAT WEEK'S SHOPPING LIST.

SCHEDULES: A WEEK'S WORTH OF DINNERS AT A GLANCE.
USE THE COLUMN MARKED "YOUR ALTERNATIVE" TO
CHANGE ANY RECIPE TO ONE OF YOUR CHOOSING. THIS
WAY YOU CAN MAKE CHANGES AND STILL USE THE
BASIC SCHEDULE. (DO NOT TEAR THESE OUT DURING
USE.)

SHOPPING LISTS: VERY IMPORTANT— IF YOU MAKE ANY
CHANGES TO THE WEEKLY SCHEDULE, YOU MUST
MAKE THE APPROPRIATE CHANGES TO YOUR
SHOPPING LIST FOR THAT WEEK. DELETE ANY
INGREDIENTS THAT THE CANCELLED RECIPE NEEDED
(CHECK OTHER RECIPES FOR THAT WEEK TO BE SURE
PART OF THE INGREDIENTS ARE NOT NEEDED) AND

ADD ITEMS NECESSARY FOR YOUR REPLACEMENT RECIPE. WE HAVE ENCLOSED 3 COPIES OF EACH SHOPPING LIST SO THEY CAN BE TORN OUT AND BROUGHT TO THE STORE. WE RECOMMEND THAT YOU <u>NOT</u> TEAR OUT THE THIRD COPY; USE IT, INSTEAD, FOR FUTURE REFERENCE.

ON THE BACK OF THE SHOPPING LISTS THAT YOU <u>CAN</u> TAKE TO THE STORE THERE IS SPACE PROVIDED FOR ADDITIONAL ITEMS YOU MAY NEED (TOILETRIES, PET FOOD, ETC.)

TEAR OUT SHOPPING LISTS, NOT SCHEDULES.

BASIC EQUIPMENT

The following is a list of all equipment you will need to prepare any recipe in this book. Here's what to do: take the biggest, fattest marker you can find and cross off each item you already have (you probably have most) - now just buy the rest and you're ready to start cooking!

baking pan (at least 9" x 12")
2 frying pans (at least 1 lid)
broiling pan
large pot (at least 2 quarts) with lid
2 sauce pans (small pots)
2 mixing bowls
2 shallow bowls (salad bowls will do)
measuring cup
measuring spoon
collander (drainer)
spatula
cutting board
knife, large
fork·
steamer (collapsible metal basket)
can opener
grater
peeler
wind-up kitchen timer (optional)

BE SURE TO REGULARLY CHECK YOUR BASIC SHOPPING LIST STOCK.

BASIC SHOPPING LIST - DO NOT TEAR OUT!

These items are used most often in our recipes.
The majority you have to buy only once every few months.
Be sure to watch your stock to replenish as needed.

S = store on shelf   R = store in refrigerator

R - catsup
R - eggs (brown or white, jumbo)
R - lemon juice
R - margarine or butter
R - mayonnaise
R - mustard (dark brown)
R - Parmesan cheese (grated)
R - relish, sweet pickle
S - bread crumbs, seasoned
S - flour
S - honey (a large can or jar can
     last more than a year on shelf)
S - paper towels
S - plastic wrap (large)
S - soy sauce

S - spaghetti (large)
S - teriyaki sauce
S - tin foil (large)
S - vegetable oil
S - vinegar (red wine, preferable)
S - Worcestershire sauce

Spices/herbs (shelf):
basil
curry powder
dill
garlic powder
ginger powder
paprika

MEAL SCHEDULES ALLOW YOU THE TIME TO DO WHAT'S REALLY IMPORTANT:
EATING!

WEEK 1

Day	Entree	pg.	Side Dish	pg.	Salad	pg.	Your Alternative
1	Honey Chicken	86	Steamed Carrots	150	Apple-Celery Salad	169	
2	Fettucine	118	Fried Tomatoes	155	Mixed green Salad (Save 4 leaves)	164	
3	Burgers w/ a secret	106	Raw Carrot Sticks		Cole Slaw (dbl. recipe)	167	
4	Eggs n' Apples (Save ½ hotdogs)	132			Mixed green Salad	164	
5	Tuna Boat	140	Toasted English Muffins		Cole Slaw (from day 3)	167	
6	Taco Salad Save ½ chips	111			Diced Oranges		
7	Potato Chipkin	93	Buttered Noodles (left from fettucini)		Zucchini Salad	168	

SHOPPING LISTS CAN BE TORN OUT AND TAKEN TO THE SUPERMARKET.

SHOPPING LIST - WEEK 1

Quantities based on two adults

MEATS
3 lbs. chicken (best of cut-up fryer) -
   freeze half.
1-1/2 lbs. ground beef - freeze 2/3,
   refrig. remainder.
1 pkg. hot dogs
1 can, 9-1/2 oz., tuna
   (white albacore is best)

VEGETABLES/FRUITS
2 oranges
1 avocado (to ripen in 5 days - if not
   ripe by fourth day, place in
   paper bag overnight.)
4 large tomatoes
2 med. onions

2 med. mushrooms
   (more if you desire for salads)
2 med. red apples
1 pkg. carrots
1 large head lettuce (& favorite
   salad ingredients for 2 meals)
1 small head cabbage
2 med. zucchini
1 bunch celery

DAIRY
1 pint heavy cream
1 lb. pkg. Cheddar cheese

GRAIN
1 pkg. English muffins
1 pkg., 12 oz., flat medium noodles

MISC.
1 med. pkg. potato chips
1 med. pkg. corn chips
1 sm. pkg. taco seasoning mix
1 bottle French dressing

ADDITIONAL ITEMS

SHOPPING LIST - WEEK 1

Quantities based on two adults

MEATS
3 lbs. chicken (best of cut-up fryer) -
   freeze half.
1-1/2 lbs. ground beef - freeze 2/3,
   refrig. remainder.
1 pkg. hot dogs
1 can, 9-1/2 oz., tuna
   (white albacore is best)

VEGETABLES/FRUITS
2 oranges
1 avocado (to ripen in 5 days - if not
   ripe by fourth day, place in
   paper bag overnight.)
4 large tomatoes
2 med. onions

2 med. mushrooms
   (more if you desire for salads)
2 med. red apples
1 pkg. carrots
1 large head lettuce (& favorite
   salad ingredients for 2 meals)
1 small head cabbage
2 med. zucchini
1 bunch celery

DAIRY
1 pint heavy cream
1 lb. pkg. Cheddar cheese

GRAIN
1 pkg. English muffins
1 pkg., 12 oz., flat medium noodles

MISC.
1 med. pkg. potato chips
1 med. pkg. corn chips
1 sm. pkg. taco seasoning mix
1 bottle French dressing

ADDITIONAL ITEMS

SHOPPING LIST - WEEK 1
(DO NOT TEAR OUT)

Quantities based on two adults

MEATS

3 lbs. chicken (best of cut-up fryer) -
   freeze half.
1-1/2 lbs. ground beef - freeze 2/3,
   refrig. remainder.
1 pkg. hot dogs
1 can, 9-1/2 oz., tuna
   (white albacore is best)

VEGETABLES/FRUITS

2 oranges
1 avocado (to ripen in 5 days - if not
   ripe by fourth day, place in
   paper bag overnight.)
4 large tomatoes
2 med. onions

2 med. mushrooms
   (more if you desire for salads)
2 med. red apples
1 pkg. carrots
1 large head lettuce (& favorite
   salad ingredients for 2 meals)
1 small head cabbage
2 med. zucchini
1 bunch celery

DAIRY

1 pint heavy cream
1 lb. pkg. Cheddar cheese

GRAIN

1 pkg. English muffins
1 pkg., 12 oz., flat medium noodles

MISC.
1 med. pkg. potato chips
1 med. pkg. corn chips
1 sm. pkg. taco seasoning mix
1 bottle French dressing

MEAL SCHEDULES ARE EASY TO USE. YOU DON'T HAVE TO DO THE PLANNING.

WEEK 2

Day	Entree	pg.	Side Dish	pg.	Salad	pg.	Your Alternative
1	Basic Hamburger w/the works	101	Toasted Corn Chips		Sauteed Mushrooms	151	
2	Spaghetti Carbonara	117	Cheesy Tomato	158	Lettuce Leaf salad w/oil & vinegar	164 & 171	
3	Oriental Chicken	96	Rice (pkg. directions)		Sauteed Snow Peas	151	
4	Broiled Fish Italiano	138	Parslied Carrots	159	Boiled Potatoes	161	
5	Hot Dogs	175	Raw carrot sticks		Creamy Cucumber Salad	170	
6	Eggs Bennie	133			Mixed Green Salad	164	
7	Pasta Salad	120	Sauteed Zucchini Tomatoes	152			

SHOPPING LISTS ELIMINATE REPEATED VISITS TO THE SUPERMARKET

SHOPPING LIST - WEEK 2

Quantities based on two adults

MEATS
1/2 lb. ground beef - refrigerate
1 small pkg. bacon
1-1/2 lbs. chicken (best of cut-up
  fryer) - freeze.
1 lb. fillet of white fish (i.e., sole,
  flounder, etc.) - freeze.
1 pkg. hot dogs (if not left over
  from week 1)

VEGETABLES/FRUITS
3 med. onions
1 green bell pepper
7 med. tomatoes
1 pkg. carrots (at least 8)
1 bunch celery
1 med. zucchini
1 lg. cucumber
1 lb. mushrooms
1 lg. head lettuce (& favorite salad
  ingredients for 1 meal)

1/2 lb. snow peas
2 white or red potatoes
1 bunch parsley
1 can, 20 oz., pineapple, chunky

DAIRY
1 lb. pkg. Cheddar

GRAIN
1 box croutons
1 pkg. hamburger buns (freeze
  remainder after meal)
1 pkg. hot dog buns (freeze
  remainder after meal)
1 pkg. pasta (curls, shells, etc.)
1 pkg. English muffins (if not left
  over from week 1)
1 pkg. brown or white rice (buy
  large package to last)

MISC.
1 pkg. corn chips (unless leftover)
1 sm. bottle Italian dressing

SHOPPING LIST - WEEK 2

Quantities based on two adults

MEATS
1/2 lb. ground beef - refrigerate
1 small pkg. bacon
1-1/2 lbs. chicken (best of cut-up
    fryer) - freeze.
1 lb. fillet of white fish (i.e., sole,
    flounder, etc.) - freeze.
1 pkg. hot dogs (if not left over
    from week 1)

VEGETABLES/FRUITS
3 med. onions
1 green bell pepper
7 med. tomatoes
1 pkg. carrots (at least 8)
1 bunch celery
1 med. zucchini
1 lg. cucumber
1 lb. mushrooms
1 lg. head lettuce (& favorite salad
    ingredients for 1 meal)

1/2 lb. snow peas
2 white or red potatoes
1 bunch parsley
1 can, 20 oz., pineapple, chunky

DAIRY
1 lb. pkg. Cheddar

GRAIN
1 box croutons
1 pkg. hamburger buns (freeze
    remainder after meal)
1 pkg. hot dog buns (freeze
    remainder after meal)
1 pkg. pasta (curls, shells, etc.)
1 pkg. English muffins (if not left
    over from week 1)
1 pkg. brown or white rice (buy
    large package to last)

MISC.
1 pkg. corn chips (unless leftover)
1 sm. bottle Italian dressing

SHOPPING LIST - WEEK 2
(DO NOT TEAR OUT)

Quantities based on two adults

MEATS
1/2 lb. ground beef - refrigerate
1 small pkg. bacon
1-1/2 lbs. chicken (best of cut-up
    fryer) - freeze.
1 lb. fillet of white fish (i.e., sole,
    flounder, etc.) - freeze.
1 pkg. hot dogs (if not left over
    from week 1)

VEGETABLES/FRUITS
3 med. onions
1 green bell pepper
7 med. tomatoes
1 pkg. carrots (at least 8)
1 bunch celery
1 med. zucchini
1 lg. cucumber
1 lb. mushrooms
1 lg. head lettuce (& favorite salad
    ingredients for 1 meal)

1/2 lb. snow peas
2 white or red potatoes
1 bunch parsley
1 can, 20 oz., pineapple, chunky

DAIRY
1 lb. pkg. Cheddar

GRAIN
1 box croutons
1 pkg. hamburger buns (freeze
    remainder after meal)
1 pkg. hot dog buns (freeze
    remainder after meal)
1 pkg. pasta (curls, shells, etc.)
1 pkg. English muffins (if not left
    over from week 1)
1 pkg. brown or white rice (buy
    large package to last)

MISC.
1 pkg. corn chips (unless leftover)
1 sm. bottle Italian dressing

MEAL SCHEDULES ORGANIZE YOUR DINNERS.

WEEK 3

Day	Entree	pg.	Side Dish	pg.	Salad	pg.	Your Alternative
1	Curried Chicken	87	Rice (pkg. directions)		Sauteed Zucchini	152	
2	Mushroom Omelette	128 & 129	Toasted English Muffins		Avocado/ Papaya Salad	165	
3	Spaghetti Aglio e olio	116	Eggplant Pizza	156	Lettuce Leaf salad w/croutons	164	
4	Sloppy Joes	110	Steamed Green Beans	150			
5	Salmon Croquettes	145	Buttered Noodles (pkg. directions)		Steamed Carrots	150	
6	Lemon Chicken	95	Dinner rolls (pkg. directions)		Steamed Broccoli	150	
7	Lasagna	121			Zucchini Salad	168	

DON'T GET CAUGHT SHORT – SHOPPING LISTS GIVE YOU AN ENTIRE WEEK'S WORTH OF DINNERS.

SHOPPING LIST - WEEK 3

Quantities based on two adults.

MEATS
3 lbs. chicken (best of cut-up fryer) -
     divide into 2 equal pkgs.,
     freeze one.
1-1/2 lbs. ground beef - divide in
     two pkgs.- 2/3 and 1/3.
     Freeze both.
1 can, 15-1/2 oz., red salmon

VEGETABLES/FRUITS
1/4 lb. mushrooms
1 med. onion
1 med. eggplant
1/2 lb. green beans
4 med. zucchini
1 ripe papaya
1 ripe avocado
1 head lettuce
1 pkg. carrots

MISC.
1 sm. bottle chili sauce
2 lb. jar of spaghetti sauce
1 lb. jar of spaghetti sauce

3/4 lb. broccoli
1 bunch parsley

DAIRY
1 pint milk
1 lb. Ricotta cheese
2 lbs. Mozzarella cheese

GRAIN
1 lb. box lasagna noodles
1 pkg., 12 oz., flat medium noodles
1 pkg. English muffins (unless
     leftover from week 1)
1 pkg. dinner rolls - brown & serve
     variety (freeze uncooked)
1 pkg. seasoned bread crumbs (buy
     large pkg. to last)
1 pkg. rice (unless leftover)
1 box croutons (unless leftover)

ADDITIONAL ITEMS

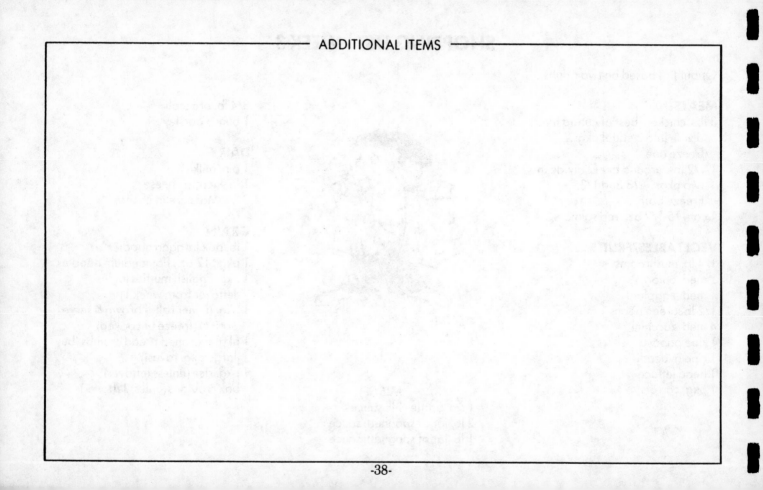

SHOPPING LIST - WEEK 3

Quantities based on two adults.

MEATS

3 lbs. chicken (best of cut-up fryer) - divide into 2 equal pkgs., freeze one.

1-1/2 lbs. ground beef - divide in two pkgs.- 2/3 and 1/3. Freeze both.

1 can, 15-1/2 oz., red salmon

VEGETABLES/FRUITS

1/4 lb. mushrooms
1 med. onion
1 med. eggplant
1/2 lb. green beans
4 med. zucchini
1 ripe papaya
1 ripe avocado
1 head lettuce
1 pkg. carrots

MISC.

1 sm. bottle chili sauce
2 lb. jar of spaghetti sauce
1 lb. jar of spaghetti sauce

3/4 lb. broccoli
1 bunch parsley

DAIRY

1 pint milk
1 lb. Ricotta cheese
2 lbs. Mozzarella cheese

GRAIN

1 lb. box lasagna noodles
1 pkg., 12 oz., flat medium noodles
1 pkg. English muffins (unless leftover from week 1)
1 pkg. dinner rolls - brown & serve variety (freeze uncooked)
1 pkg. seasoned bread crumbs (buy large pkg. to last)
1 pkg. rice (unless leftover)
1 box croutons (unless leftover)

SHOPPING LIST - WEEK 3
(DO NOT TEAR OUT)

Quantities based on two adults.

MEATS
3 lbs. chicken (best of cut-up fryer) -
    divide into 2 equal pkgs.,
    freeze one.
1-1/2 lbs. ground beef - divide in
    two pkgs.- 2/3 and 1/3.
    Freeze both.
1 can, 15-1/2 oz., red salmon

VEGETABLES/FRUITS
1/4 lb. mushrooms
1 med. onion
1 med. eggplant
1/2 lb. green beans
4 med. zucchini
1 ripe papaya
1 ripe avocado
1 head lettuce
1 pkg. carrots

MISC.
1 sm. bottle chili sauce
2 lb. jar of spaghetti sauce
1 lb. jar of spaghetti sauce

3/4 lb. broccoli
1 bunch parsley

DAIRY
1 pint milk
1 lb. Ricotta cheese
2 lbs. Mozzarella cheese

GRAIN
1 lb. box lasagna noodles
1 pkg., 12 oz., flat medium noodles
1 pkg. English muffins (unless
    leftover from week 1)
1 pkg. dinner rolls - brown & serve
    variety (freeze uncooked)
1 pkg. seasoned bread crumbs (buy
    large pkg. to last)
1 pkg. rice (unless leftover)
1 box croutons (unless leftover)

MEAL SCHEDULES ALLOW YOU TO CHOOSE ALTERNATIVES.

WEEK 4

Day	Entree	pg.	Side Dish	pg.	Salad	pg.	Your Alternative
1	Ginger Beef	107	Orange Slices		Creamy Cucumber Salad	170	
2	Shrimp Salad	139	Garlic Bread	179	Diced Oranges		
3	Curried Cream Eggs	131	Sliced Apples		Zucchini Salad	168	
4	Lasagna	121			Mixed Green Salad	168	
5	Avocado Cheeseburger	103	Home Fries	161		164	
6	Chicken & Garlic	92	Rice (pkg. directions)		Mixed Green Salad	164	
7	Fish with Mustard Sauce	144	Steamed Asparagus	150	Dinner rolls (pkg. directions)		

SHOPPING LISTS CAN BE CHANGED WHEN YOU CHANGE SCHEDULES.

SHOPPING LIST - WEEK 4

Quantities based on two adults.

MEAT
1-1/2 lbs. ground beef - divide into
   1 lb. pkg. & 1/2 lb. pkg. & freeze
   1/2 lb.
1/2 lb. small cooked shrimp -
   refrigerate.
4 chicken breasts, boned - freeze.
1 lb. boneless fillet of fish (haddock,
   cod, etc.)

VEGETABLES/FRUITS
3 med. tomatoes
1 med. onion
1 avocado (to ripen in 5 days)
2 med. cucumber
1 bunch parsley
1 red apple
4 oranges
2 baking potatoes

1 lg. head of lettuce (& favorite
   salad ingredients for 2 meals)
2 med. zucchini
1 bunch (8 stalks) asparagus (frozen
   or canned if fresh is unavailable)

DAIRY
1/2 pint heavy cream
1 pint milk
1 sm. pkg. firm cheese, i.e.,
   Cheddar, Monterey Jack, etc.

GRAIN
1 pkg. English muffins
   (unless leftover)
1 loaf French or sourdough bread,
   hard crust (freeze 1/2)
1 pkg dinner rolls - brown & serve
   variety (unless leftover)
1 pkg. rice (unless leftover)

SHOPPING LIST - WEEK 4

Quantities based on two adults.

MEAT
1-1/2 lbs. ground beef - divide into
    1 lb. pkg. & 1/2 lb. pkg. & freeze
    1/2 lb.
1/2 lb. small cooked shrimp -
    refrigerate.
4 chicken breasts, boned - freeze.
1 lb. boneless fillet of fish (haddock,
    cod, etc.)

VEGETABLES/FRUITS
3 med. tomatoes
1 med. onion
1 avocado (to ripen in 5 days)
2 med. cucumber
1 bunch parsley
1 red apple
4 oranges
2 baking potatoes

1 lg. head of lettuce (& favorite
    salad ingredients for 2 meals)
2 med. zucchini
1 bunch (8 stalks) asparagus (frozen
    or canned if fresh is unavailable)

DAIRY
1/2 pint heavy cream
1 pint milk
1 sm. pkg. firm cheese, i.e.,
    Cheddar, Monterey Jack, etc.

GRAIN
1 pkg. English muffins
    (unless leftover)
1 loaf French or sourdough bread,
    hard crust (freeze 1/2)
1 pkg dinner rolls - brown & serve
    variety (unless leftover)
1 pkg. rice (unless leftover)

SHOPPING LIST - WEEK 4
(DO NOT TEAR OUT)

Quantities based on two adults.

MEAT
1-1/2 lbs. ground beef - divide into
    1 lb. pkg. & 1/2 lb. pkg. & freeze
    1/2 lb.
1/2 lb. small cooked shrimp -
    refrigerate.
4 chicken breasts, boned - freeze.
1 lb. boneless fillet of fish (haddock,
    cod, etc.)

VEGETABLES/FRUITS
3 med. tomatoes
1 med. onion
1 avocado (to ripen in 5 days)
2 med. cucumber
1 bunch parsley
1 red apple
4 oranges
2 baking potatoes

1 lg. head of lettuce (& favorite
    salad ingredients for 2 meals)
2 med. zucchini
1 bunch (8 stalks) asparagus (frozen
    or canned if fresh is unavailable)

DAIRY
1/2 pint heavy cream
1 pint milk
1 sm. pkg. firm cheese, i.e.,
    Cheddar, Monterey Jack, etc.

GRAIN
1 pkg. English muffins
    (unless leftover)
1 loaf French or sourdough bread,
    hard crust (freeze 1/2)
1 pkg dinner rolls - brown & serve
    variety (unless leftover)
1 pkg. rice (unless leftover)

MEAL SCHEDULES OFFER A BALANCED DIET.

WEEK 5

Day	Entree	pg.	Side Dish	pg.	Salad	pg.	Your Alternative
1	Orange Chicken	88	Stuffed shirt Potatoes	160	Steamed Broccoli	150	
2	Baked Spaghetti	115			Mixed Green Salad	164	
3	Scrambled Eggs w/onion	126	Sliced Avocado		Fruit Salad	166	
4	Bouillabaise	141	Steamed Winter Squash	152			
5	Creamy Macaroni	119	Parslied Carrots	159	Sliced Cucumber		
6	Bouillabaise (from Day 4)	(141)			Mixed Green Salad	164	
7	Chicken Paprika	94	Mashed Potatoes	161	Steamed Artichoke	150	

YOU GET THREE COPIES OF EACH SHOPPING LIST.

SHOPPING LIST - WEEK 5

Quantities based on two adults.

MEATS
3 lbs. chicken (best of cut-up fryer) -
    divide into 2 equal pkgs.,
    freeze one.
1 lb. boneless white fish fillet -
    freeze.

VEGETABLES/FRUITS
2 med. onions
1 bunch celery
3 baking potatoes
1 large winter squash (i.e.,
    butternut, acorn, etc.)
1 pkg. carrots
3/4 lb. broccoli

1 lg. head of lettuce (& favorite
    salad ingredients for 2 meals)
1 lb. selection of 3 favorite fruits
    (for salad)
2 artichokes
1 avocado (to ripen in 3 days)
1 med. cucumber
1 bunch parsley

DAIRY
1 6 oz. container sour cream

GRAIN
1 lb. box macaroni noodles

MISC.
1 can, 10 oz., frozen orange
juice concentrate
1 can, 28 oz. concentrated
cooked tomatoes
1 lb. jar of spaghetti sauce

SHOPPING LIST - WEEK 5

Quantities based on two adults.

MEATS
3 lbs. chicken (best of cut-up fryer) -
   divide into 2 equal pkgs.,
   freeze one.
1 lb. boneless white fish fillet -
   freeze.

VEGETABLES/FRUITS
2 med. onions
1 bunch celery
3 baking potatoes
1 large winter squash (i.e.,
   butternut, acorn, etc.)
1 pkg. carrots
3/4 lb. broccoli

1 lg. head of lettuce (& favorite
   salad ingredients for 2 meals)
1 lb. selection of 3 favorite fruits
   (for salad)
2 artichokes
1 avocado (to ripen in 3 days)
1 med. cucumber
1 bunch parsley

DAIRY
1 6 oz. container sour cream

GRAIN
1 lb. box macaroni noodles

MISC.
1 can, 10 oz., frozen orange
juice concentrate
1 can, 28 oz. concentrated
cooked tomatoes
1 lb. jar of spaghetti sauce

SHOPPING LIST - WEEK 5

(DO NOT TEAR OUT)

Quantities based on two adults.

MEATS

3 lbs. chicken (best of cut-up fryer) -
   divide into 2 equal pkgs.,
   freeze one.
1 lb. boneless white fish fillet -
   freeze.

VEGETABLES/FRUITS

2 med. onions
1 bunch celery
3 baking potatoes
1 large winter squash (i.e.,
   butternut, acorn, etc.)
1 pkg. carrots
3/4 lb. broccoli

1 lg. head of lettuce (& favorite
   salad ingredients for 2 meals)
1 lb. selection of 3 favorite fruits
   (for salad)
2 artichokes
1 avocado (to ripen in 3 days)
1 med. cucumber
1 bunch parsley

DAIRY

1 6 oz. container sour cream

GRAIN

1 lb. box macaroni noodles

MISC.

1 can, 10 oz., frozen orange
juice concentrate
1 can, 28 oz. concentrated
cooked tomatoes
1 lb. jar of spaghetti sauce

MEAL SCHEDULES ARE ECONOMICAL.

WEEK 6

Day	Entree	pg.	Side Dish	pg.	Salad	pg.	Your Alternative
1	Barbecued Spareribs	176	Corn on the cob	151	Steamed Cauliflower	150	
2	Open Hamburger	104	Fried Tomatoes	155	Mixed Green Salad	164	
3	Cheese Omelette	128 & 129	Toasted English Muffins		Fruit Salad	166	
4	Teriyaki Burger	105			Cole slaw (dbl. recipe)	167	
5	Gina Lola Chickena	89	Garlic Bread	179	Mixed Green Salad	164	
6	Lasagna	(121)	Sauteed Mushrooms	151	Raw, cut up Cauliflower w/Russian Dressing	150	
7	Chicken Soup	91	Crackers		Cole slaw (from day 4)	(167)	

SHOPPING LISTS ELIMINATE HAVING TO PLAN AHEAD.

SHOPPING LIST - WEEK 6

Quantities based on two adults.

MEATS
1 lb. ground beef - freeze 1/2.
3 lb. stewing chicken - freeze after
   removing giblets.
1-1/2 lbs. frying chicken (best of
   cut-up fryer)-freeze.
6 - 8 pork spareribs - refrigerate.

VEGETABLES/FRUITS
1 pkg. carrots
1 sm. head cauliflower
4 small onions
1 green bell pepper
1 bunch celery
1 bunch parsley
2 med. tomatoes
1 lg. head of lettuce (& favorite
   salad ingredients for 2 meals)
1 lb. selection of 3 favorite fruits
   (for Fruit Salad)

1 head cabbage
2 ears corn (frozen corn, if fresh
   not available)
1 lb. mushrooms
1 can, 16 oz., stewed tomatoes

DAIRY
1 pkg. firm cheese, i.e., Cheddar,
   Monterey Jack, etc.

GRAIN
1 loaf white or wheat bread
   (freeze unused)
1 loaf French or sourdough bread,
   hard crust (unless leftover)
1 pkg. English muffins
   (unless leftover)
1 pkg. crackers (for Chicken
   Soup meal)

MISC.
1 can, 16 oz. stewed tomatoes

ADDITIONAL ITEMS

-62-

SHOPPING LIST - WEEK 6

Quantities based on two adults.

MEATS
1 lb. ground beef - freeze 1/2.
3 lb. stewing chicken - freeze after
   removing giblets.
1-1/2 lbs. frying chicken (best of
   cut-up fryer)-freeze.
6 - 8 pork spareribs - refrigerate.

VEGETABLES/FRUITS
1 pkg. carrots
1 sm. head cauliflower
4 small onions
1 green bell pepper
1 bunch celery
1 bunch parsley
2 med. tomatoes
1 lg. head of lettuce (& favorite
   salad ingredients for 2 meals)
1 lb.selection of 3 favorite fruits
   (for Fruit Salad)

1 head cabbage
2 ears corn (frozen corn, if fresh
   not available)
1 lb. mushrooms
1 can, 16 oz., stewed tomatoes

DAIRY
1 pkg. firm cheese, i.e., Cheddar,
   Monterey Jack, etc.

GRAIN
1 loaf white or wheat bread
   (freeze unused)
1 loaf French or sourdough bread,
   hard crust (unless leftover)
1 pkg. English muffins
   (unless leftover)
1 pkg. crackers (for Chicken
   Soup meal)

MISC.
1 can, 16 oz. stewed tomatoes

ADDITIONAL ITEMS

SHOPPING LIST - WEEK 6
(DO NOT TEAR OUT)

Quantities based on two adults.

MEATS
1 lb. ground beef - freeze 1/2.
3 lb. stewing chicken - freeze after
  removing giblets.
1-1/2 lbs. frying chicken (best of
  cut-up fryer)-freeze.
6 - 8 pork spareribs - refrigerate.

VEGETABLES/FRUITS
1 pkg. carrots
1 sm. head cauliflower
4 small onions
1 green bell pepper
1 bunch celery
1 bunch parsley
2 med. tomatoes
1 lg. head of lettuce (& favorite
  salad ingredients for 2 meals)
1 lb. selection of 3 favorite fruits
  (for Fruit Salad)

1 head cabbage
2 ears corn (frozen corn, if fresh
  not available)
1 lb. mushrooms
1 can, 16 oz., stewed tomatoes

DAIRY
1 pkg. firm cheese, i.e., Cheddar,
  Monterey Jack, etc.

GRAIN
1 loaf white or wheat bread
  (freeze unused)
1 loaf French or sourdough bread,
  hard crust (unless leftover)
1 pkg. English muffins
  (unless leftover)
1 pkg. crackers (for Chicken
  Soup meal)

MISC.
1 can, 16 oz. stewed tomatoes

-65-

MEAL SCHEDULES KEEP YOU OUT OF FAST FOOD RESTAURANTS.

WEEK 7

Day	Entree	pg.	Side Dish	pg.	Salad	pg.	Your Alternative
1	Eggplant Pizza (save ½ eggplant)	156	Buttered Noodles (pkg. directions)		Mixed Green Salad	164	
2	Chicken Soup (from Day 7)	(91)	Fried zucchini Circles	157			
3	Broccoli Burger	109	Rice (pkg. directions)		Fried Tomatoes	155	
4	Fish Dressed in White	143	Steamed Broccoli	150	Apple & Celery Salad	169	
5	Lasagna	(121)	Sauteed Eggplant & Onion w/garlic	151			
6	Fried Chicken	90	Mashed Potatoes	161	Mixed Green Salad	164	
7	Breaded Pork chops	177	Steamed Green Beans	150	Applesauce (store bought)		

SHOPPING LISTS CUT DOWN ON IMPULSE BUYING.

SHOPPING LIST - WEEK 7

Quantities based on two adults.

MEATS
1/2 lb. ground beef - freeze.
1-1/2 lbs. chicken (best of cut-up fryer) - freeze.
4 pork chops (approx. 1/2" thick) - freeze.
1 lb. boneless fillet of fish (haddock, cod, etc.) - freeze.

VEGETABLES/FRUITS
1 lg. eggplant
1-1/2 lbs. broccoli
2 med. zucchini
2 potatoes
1/2 lb. green beans
1 lg. head of lettuce (& favorite salad ingredients for 2 meals)

2 tomatoes
1 bunch celery
1 red apple
1 bunch parsley
1 med. onion
1 sm. jar applesauce

DAIRY
1 pint milk
1 pkg., 6 oz., sour cream
1 sm. pkg. Mozzarella

GRAIN
1 pkg. flat medium noodles
1 pkg. white or brown rice (unless leftover)

MISC.
1 sm. jar spaghetti sauce

SHOPPING LIST - WEEK 7

Quantities based on two adults.

MEATS
1/2 lb. ground beef - freeze.
1-1/2 lbs. chicken (best of cut-up
   fryer) - freeze.
4 pork chops (approx. 1/2'' thick) -
   freeze.
1 lb. boneless fillet of fish (haddock,
   cod, etc.) - freeze.

VEGETABLES/FRUITS
1 lg. eggplant
1-1/2 lbs. broccoli
2 med. zucchini
2 potatoes
1/2 lb. green beans
1 lg. head of lettuce (& favorite
   salad ingredients for 2 meals)

2 tomatoes
1 bunch celery
1 red apple
1 bunch parsley
1 med. onion
1 sm. jar applesauce

DAIRY
1 pint milk
1 pkg., 6 oz., sour cream
1 sm. pkg. Mozzarella

GRAIN
1 pkg. flat medium noodles
1 pkg. white or brown rice
   (unless leftover)

MISC.
1 sm. jar spaghetti sauce

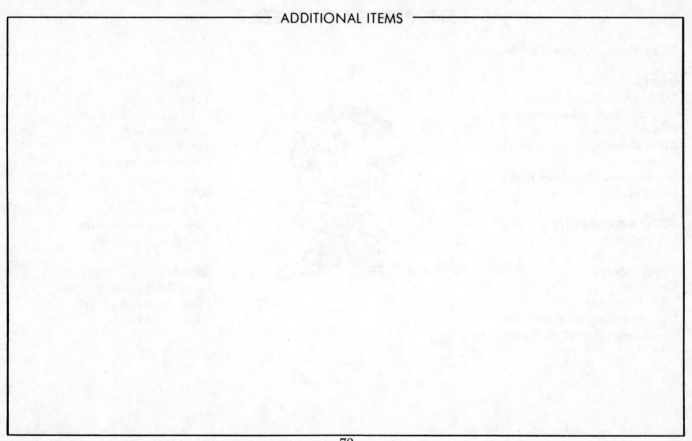

ADDITIONAL ITEMS

SHOPPING LIST - WEEK 7
(DO NOT TEAR OUT)

Quantities based on two adults.

MEATS
1/2 lb. ground beef - freeze.
1-1/2 lbs. chicken (best of cut-up fryer) - freeze.
4 pork chops (approx. 1/2" thick) - freeze.
1 lb. boneless fillet of fish (haddock, cod, etc.) - freeze.

VEGETABLES/FRUITS
1 lg. eggplant
1-1/2 lbs. broccoli
2 med. zucchini
2 potatoes
1/2 lb. green beans
1 lg. head of lettuce (& favorite salad ingredients for 2 meals)

2 tomatoes
1 bunch celery
1 red apple
1 bunch parsley
1 med. onion
1 sm. jar applesauce

DAIRY
1 pint milk
1 pkg., 6 oz., sour cream
1 sm. pkg. Mozzarella

GRAIN
1 pkg. flat medium noodles
1 pkg. white or brown rice (unless leftover)

MISC.
1 sm. jar spaghetti sauce

MEAL SCHEDULES OFFER A WIDE VARIETY OF FOODS.

WEEK 8

Day	Entree	pg.	Side Dish	pg.	Salad	pg.	Your Alternative
1	Sour cream & Tomato Omelette	128 & 129	Toasted English Muffins		Fruit salad	166	
2	Fish & Dip	142	Steamed Butternut Squash	152	Cole Slaw (Dbl. recipe)	167	
3	Pasta salad	120	Garlic bread	179	Sliced Oranges		
4	Meat & Potatoes	108	Steamed Green Beans	150	Mixed Green Salad	164	
5	Broiled Cheese & Tuna sandwich	140 A	Raw celery sticks		Creamy Cucumber Salad	170	
6	BBQ Chicken	97	Corn on the Cob	151	Cole slaw (from day 2)	167	
7	A TREAT! Porterhouse Steak	178	Baked potato w/sour cream	161	Mixed Green Salad	164	

SHOPPING LISTS SPEED UP SHOPPING.

SHOPPING LIST - WEEK 8

Quantities based on two adults

MEATS
3/4 lb. ground beef - refrigerate.
1 can, 9 1/2 oz. tuna fish
1-1/2 lbs. chicken - freeze.
2 porterhouse steaks - freeze.
1 lb. boneless fillet of fish (haddock,
    cod, etc.) - refrigerate.

VEGETABLES/FRUITS
3 tomatoes
2 med. onions
1 bunch celery
4 baking potatoes
1/2 lb. green beans
2 ears corn (or frozen)
1 lb. selection of 3 favorite fruits
2 oranges
1 carrot

1 lg. head of lettuce (& favorite
    salad ingredients for 2 meals)
1 large cucumber
1 sm. head cabbage
1 med. butternut squash

DAIRY
1/2 pint heavy cream
1 container, 6 oz., sour cream
1 pkg. firm cheese, i.e., Cheddar,
    Monterey Jack, etc.

GRAIN
1 pkg. pasta (curls, shells, etc.)
1 pkg. English muffins (unless
    leftover)
1 loaf French or sourdough bread,
    hard crust (unless leftover)

MISC.
1 small can corn (optional)

SHOPPING LIST - WEEK 8

Quantities based on two adults

MEATS
3/4 lb. ground beef - refrigerate.
1 can, 9 1/2 oz. tuna fish
1-1/2 lbs. chicken - freeze.
2 porterhouse steaks - freeze.
1 lb. boneless fillet of fish (haddock, cod, etc.) - refrigerate.

VEGETABLES/FRUITS
3 tomatoes
2 med. onions
1 bunch celery
4 baking potatoes
1/2 lb. green beans
2 ears corn (or frozen)
1 lb. selection of 3 favorite fruits
2 oranges
1 carrot

1 lg. head of lettuce (& favorite salad ingredients for 2 meals)
1 large cucumber
1 sm. head cabbage
1 med. butternut squash

DAIRY
1/2 pint heavy cream
1 container, 6 oz., sour cream
1 pkg. firm cheese, i.e., Cheddar, Monterey Jack, etc.

GRAIN
1 pkg. pasta (curls, shells, etc.)
1 pkg. English muffins (unless leftover)
1 loaf French or sourdough bread, hard crust (unless leftover)

MISC.
1 small can corn (optional)

SHOPPING LIST - WEEK 8
(DO NOT TEAR OUT)

Quantities based on two adults

MEATS
3/4 lb. ground beef - refrigerate.
1 can, 9 1/2 oz. tuna fish
1-1/2 lbs. chicken - freeze.
2 porterhouse steaks - freeze.
1 lb. boneless fillet of fish (haddock, cod, etc.) - refrigerate.

VEGETABLES/FRUITS
3 tomatoes
2 med. onions
1 bunch celery
4 baking potatoes
1/2 lb. green beans
2 ears corn (or frozen)
1 lb. selection of 3 favorite fruits
2 oranges
1 carrot

1 lg. head of lettuce (& favorite salad ingredients for 2 meals)
1 large cucumber
1 sm. head cabbage
1 med. butternut squash

DAIRY
1/2 pint heavy cream
1 container, 6 oz., sour cream
1 pkg. firm cheese, i.e., Cheddar, Monterey Jack, etc.

GRAIN
1 pkg. pasta (curls, shells, etc.)
1 pkg. English muffins (unless leftover)
1 loaf French or sourdough bread, hard crust (unless leftover)

MISC.
1 small can corn (optional)

DEAR READER,

THE SECOND HALF OF WHO <u>ME</u> COOK? IS DEDICATED TO OUR FAVORITE RECIPES. EACH ONE IS WRITTEN IN A SIMPLE AND EASY-TO-READ FORM.

WHETHER YOU ARE A BEGINNER OR A GOURMET, WE FEEL THAT YOU'LL FIND EACH RECIPE DELICIOUS WITH A MINIMUM OF PREPARATION.

WELCOME TO OUR KITCHEN. ENJOY!

Joel & Mark

AND NOW... THE RECIPES!

DON'T BE CHICKEN!

YOU <u>CAN</u> COOK DELICIOUS CHICKEN — WORTHY OF GUESTS OR JUST FOR YOU. HERE ARE SOME TIPS HOW :

UNLESS YOU WISH TO WRESTLE WITH A WHOLE BIRD, THE BEST VALUE IN CHICKEN IS THE PACKAGE MARKED "BEST OF CUT UP FRYER."

THE SLOWER CHICKEN IS COOKED THE MORE TENDER IT IS. SO, IF YOU HAVE THE TIME, LET YOUR CHICKEN COOK AT 200° OR 300° YOU CAN TELL WHEN IT IS DONE WHEN THE CHICKEN IS NO LONGER PINK INSIDE.

300° — 1½ HOURS APPROX.
200° — 2 HOURS APPROX.

IF YOU'VE FORGOTTEN TO DEFROST THE BIRD, DO NOT DESPAIR! JUST STICK IT IN THE OVEN AT 300° FOR ½ AN HOUR — IT SHOULD BE DEFROSTED AND READY FOR ANY OF THE FOLLOWING RECIPES.

HONEY CHICKEN

Preheat Oven 350°

INGREDIENTS
1-1/2 lbs. chicken
1/4 cup honey
1/4 cup mustard
1 tsp. lemon juice
salt & pepper lightly

Serves 2

EQUIPMENT
small bowl
mixing spoon
measuring cup
measuring spoon
baking pan
knife
fork

1. Combine honey, mustard, lemon, salt & pepper in bowl and mix thoroughly.
2. Pierce chicken with knife in several places.
3. Coat chicken with half of sauce.
4. Place chicken skin side down in baking pan.
5. Bake 25 mins.
6. Turn chicken and pour over rest of sauce.
7. Bake 25 mins. longer, or until no longer pink inside.

CURRIED CHICKEN

Preheat Oven 350°

Serves 2

INGREDIENTS

1-1/2 lbs. chicken
1/4 cup honey
2 Tbsp. mustard
1 tsp. curry

EQUIPMENT

small bowl
baking pan
measuring cup
measuring spoons
spoon
knife

1. Combine honey, mustard & curry in small bowl, mixing well.
2. Pierce chicken with knife in several places.
3. Coat chicken with 1/2 of the sauce.
4. Place chicken skin side down in baking pan.
5. Bake 25 mins., turn chicken and add rest of sauce.
6. Bake 25 mins. more,or until no longer pink inside.

ORANGE CHICKEN

Stove top

Serves 2

INGREDIENTS

1-1/2 lbs. chicken
1 cup orange juice
2 Tbsp. cooking oil

EQUIPMENT

frying pan
measuring cup
measuring spoon
fork
paper towels

1. Rinse chicken and pat dry with paper towels.
2. Over medium heat, brown chicken in oil, about 5 mins. each side.
3. Add 3/4 cup orange juice (if frozen first dilute as according to can directions).
4. Simmer for 20 mins. over low heat until orange juice becomes thick.
5. Add rest of orange juice and simmer another 10 mins. until orange juice is again thick forming a glaze. Chicken should no longer be pink inside.

GINA LOLA CHICKENA (A real Italian Knockout)

Preheat Oven 350°

Serves 2

INGREDIENTS

1-1/2 lbs. chicken
1 can, 16 oz., stewed
  tomatoes
1 medium onion
1 green bell pepper
1 tsp. garlic powder
1 tsp. basil
2 Tbsp. cooking oil

EQUIPMENT

baking pan
frying pan
measuring spoons
knife
spatula or fork

1. Heat oil in frying pan for 1 min. over medium flame.
2. Gently place chicken in oil and fry until lightly browned on both sides (approx. 5 mins. per side).
3. Remove chicken from frying pan and place in baking pan.
4. Seed and cut bell pepper into small pieces.
5. Peel and chop onion into small pieces.
6. Top chicken with stewed tomatoes (including juice), bell pepper and onion.
7. Sprinkle with garlic powder and basil.
8. Bake for 35 mins. or until no longer pink inside.

FRIED CHICKEN

Stove top

Serves 2

INGREDIENTS

1-1/2 lbs. chicken
1/3 cup flour
1/3 cup seasoned
    bread crumbs
1 egg
vegetable oil, as needed
2 tsp. water

EQUIPMENT

frying pan
2 plates
measuring cup
measuring spoons
shallow bowl
fork
paper towels

1. Break egg into bowl. **Add water and** beat slightly.
2. Pour bread crumbs and flour onto separate plates.
3. Wash chicken and dry with paper towels.
4. Dip one piece of chicken at a time into the flour covering both sides. Pat off excess.
5. Dip chicken into egg, coating completely.
6. Dip chicken into bread crumbs, coating completely.
7. Pour oil in pan approximately 1/2 inch deep & heat 2 mins. over medium flame.
8. Gently place chicken in oil and fry about 20 mins. Turn at least twice.
9. Drain chicken on **paper towel.**
   HINT: When cooled, **store oil in a jar** on your shelf. You can use it again to fry chicken.

JEWISH PENICILLIN (chicken soup)

Stove top

Serves 4
(or 2 for 2 meals)

INGREDIENTS

1   3 lb. stewing chicken, cut up
2   carrots
3   stalks celery
1   med. onion
1   tbsp. fresh parsley, chopped
1   tsp. garlic powder
salt & pepper to taste
1   cup egg noodles (optional)

EQUIPMENT

1 large pot with lid
measuring spoons
mixing spoon
knife
paper towels

1. Fill pot 3/4 full of water. Place over high flame.
2. Meanwhile, wash chicken under cool water and paper towel dry.
3. Wash carrots and celery.
4. Peel and slice onion thinly.
5. Chop carrots & celery into bite-size pieces.
6. Place chicken and all other ingredients in pot, reduce to simmer & cover.
7. After five mins. remove cover and, with spoon, skim off fat which is floating on surface.
8. Cover and simmer for 50 mins. You may wish to add more garlic powder, salt & pepper just before serving.

OPTIONAL: Add egg noodles to pot 10 mins. before serving.

CHICKEN & GARLIC

Stove top

Serves 2

INGREDIENTS

4 chicken breasts, boned
2 Tbsp. butter or margarine
2 Tbsp. lemon juice
1 tsp. garlic powder
2 Tbsp. fresh parsley,
   chopped fine
1/2 cup flour
salt to taste

EQUIPMENT

frying pan
plate
measuring cup
measuring spoons
spatula or fork
knife
paper towels

1. Pull & cut skin away from chicken breasts.
2. Rinse chicken under cool water and dry with paper towels.
3. Pour flour onto plate, then dip one piece of chicken at a time into flour covering both sides. Pat off excess.
4. Melt butter in frying pan over medium heat.
5. Place chicken in melted butter and sprinkle with garlic powder and salt. Cook 4 - 5 mins.
6. Finely chop parsley.
7. Turn chicken, adding parlsey and lemon juice. Continue cooking for another 4 - 5 mins. or until no longer pink inside.

POTATO CHIPKIN

Preheat Oven 350°

Serves 2

INGREDIENTS

1-1/2 lbs. chicken
1/2 cup finely crushed
    potato chips
1 egg
1 Tbsp. cream or milk
1/4 tsp. paprika
4 Tbsp. butter or margarine
pepper to taste

EQUIPMENT

baking pan
2 shallow bowls
measuring cup
measuring spoons
small plastic bag
    (paper bag will do)
fork

1. Beat egg & milk together in bowl until well blended. Set aside.
2. In small plastic bag, finely crush potato chips.
3. Melt butter in baking pan in oven. Remove from oven.
4. Mix chips & seasonings in other bowl.
5. Dip chicken in egg and then in chips, coating both sides.
6. Place in baking pan.
7. Bake 50 mins. or until no longer pink inside.

CHICKEN PAPRIKA

Preheat Oven 350°

Serves 2

INGREDIENTS

1-1/2 lbs. chicken
1 tsp. paprika
1 Tbsp. butter or margarine
salt & pepper lightly

EQUIPMENT

baking pan
measuring spoons
knife

1. Salt & pepper chicken, patting firmly.
2. Dot with butter and place in baking pan, skin side down.
3. Bake chicken 45 mins. turning once.
4. Evenly sprinkle paprika over skin side of chicken.
5. Bake 5 mins. more.

LEMON CHICKEN

Preheat oven 350°

INGREDIENTS
1-1/2 lbs. chicken
1/4 cup lemon juice
1/4 tsp. garlic powder
salt & pepper lightly

Serves 2

EQUIPMENT
baking pan
small bowl
measuring cup
measuring spoons
knife & fork

1. Salt & pepper chicken, patting firmly.
2. In bowl, combine lemon juice and garlic.
3. Pierce chicken with knife in several places.
4. Pour half of sauce over chicken.
5. Place chicken skin side down in baking pan.
6. Bake 25 mins.
7. Turn chicken and pour over rest of sauce.
8. Bake 25 mins. more or until chicken is no longer pink inside.

ORIENTAL CHICKEN

Preheat oven 350°

Serves 2

INGREDIENTS

1-1/2 lbs. chicken
1 can, 20 oz. pineapple, chunky
1 medium onion
1 stalk celery
1 green bell pepper
1 tsp. curry powder
1 tsp. ginger
1 tbsp. soy sauce

EQUIPMENT

baking pan
measuring spoons
knife
can opener

1. Place chicken skin side down in baking pan.
2. Cut bell pepper in half vertically. Break off stem and remove seeds. (You may have to rinse under cool water.)
3. Coarsely chop pepper, onion & celery.
4. Top chicken with pepper, onion, celery & pineapple (including juice).
5. Sprinkle soy sauce, curry powder and ginger over chicken, in that order.
6. Bake 50 mins. or until chicken is no longer pink inside.

BARBECUED CHICKEN

Preheat oven 350°

Serves 2

INGREDIENTS
1-1/2 lbs. chicken
1/2 cup Basic Barbecue Sauce
(p.180)

EQUIPMENT
baking pan
measuring cup
knife

1. Pierce chicken with knife in several places.
2. Prepare barbecue sauce and pour half of sauce over chicken.
3. Bake chicken 25 mins., skin side down.
4. Turn chicken and add rest of sauce, cooking 25 mins. more or until no longer pink inside.

GROUND BEEF

GROUND BEEF

BUY THE GROUND BEEF THAT YOU CAN AFFORD, KEEPING IN MIND THAT THE HIGHER THE FAT CONTENT THE MORE THE MEAT WILL SHRINK (22% FAT CONTENT IS ABOUT THE HIGHEST YOU SHOULD PURCHASE).

DO NOT STORE GROUND BEEF IN THE REFRIGERATOR FOR MORE THAN TWO DAYS.

DO NOT SLAP THE BEEF WHEN SHAPING PATTIES BECAUSE YOU WILL ONLY BE DESTROYING THE FLAVOR.

SHAPE PATTIES GENTLY, KEEPING THEM FAIRLY LOOSE.

I POUND MAKES 4 SERVINGS. PATTIES SHOULD BE ABOUT 3/4" THICK.

IT IS NOT NECESSARY TO ADD BUTTER OR ANY KIND OF OIL TO THE FRYING PAN WHEN COOKING HAMBURGERS—THE NATURAL FAT WILL GREASE THE PAN.

BASIC RULES FOR BROILING

A broiler pan has a removable tray with holes to allow drainage of the juices of your meat. This is the best type of pan to use for broiling hamburgers. On a flat pan, with no drainage, the fat is more likely to catch fire. If it does, close broiler door and turn off oven. If the fire does not burn out in a few moments, throw baking soda on it. DO NOT try to remove pan from oven.

To broil hamburgers:

1. Place patties on broiler about 3 - 4 inches beneath flame. (Pattie preparation - page 99)

2. Broil 3 mins. turn patties over, and broil 4 - 7 mins. more until desired doneness.

3. If desired, place a slice of firm cheese on patties about 15 seconds before removing them from oven.

BASIC HAMBURGER

Stove top

Serves 2

INGREDIENTS

1/2 lb. ground beef
1/4 tsp. salt
1/8 tsp. pepper
2 buns

EQUIPMENT

frying pan
baking pan
measuring spoons
spatula

1. Place buns, crust side down, in baking pan and toast in broiler for about 2 mins. Watch these - they can burn easily.
2. Form meat into 2 patties adding salt and pepper. Place patties in ungreased frying pan over medium-high heat. (don't press down with spatula) Cook 10 mins., flipping occasionally:

Approximate cooking time:

10 mins. - rare
12 mins. - medium
14 mins. - well done

Cut into patties to determine doneness.

(con't.)

BASIC HAMBURGER (Con't.)

4. Place on buns or toasted English muffins and serve.
   Some serving suggestions:

catsup	pickles (sliced)
mustard	onions (sliced)
relish	tomatoes (sliced)
Russian dressing (p. 171)	lettuce
mayonnaise	

ADDITIONS TO BASIC HAMBURGER

Add one of the following to the ground beef when forming patties (use a bowl to help mixing). Then cook as you would in the Basic Hamburger recipe or the Broiled Hamburger (p.100).

2 Tbsp. Worcestershire sauce	1/4 cup chopped onion
2 Tbsp. soy sauce, but	3/4 tsp. horseradish
eliminate salt from recipe	2 tsp. chili sauce

AVOCADO-CHEESE BURGERS

Stove top

Serves 2

INGREDIENTS

1/2 lb. ground beef
1 small avocado
1/2 cup firm cheese
    (grated or sliced)
salt & pepper lightly

EQUIPMENT

frying pan with lid
measuring cup
teaspoon
spatula
knife

1. Cut avocado in half lengthwise. Cut all the way to the pit & all the way around.
2. Chop the blade into the pit, twist and remove.
3. With the teaspoon, scoop avocado halves out of skins.
4. Slice thinly & set aside.
5. Form meat into two patties adding salt & pepper.
6. Place patties in ungreased frying pan over medium heat.
7. Cook 5 mins. - flipping occasionally.
8. Place avocado slices on each pattie. Cover and cook 2 - 3 mins.:(longer depending on your desired doneness).
9. Add cheese to top of pattie and cover, cooking 30 seconds longer or until cheese is melted. See page 102 for options.

OPEN HAMBURGER

Oven on Broil

INGREDIENTS

1/2 lb. ground beef
4 slices of bread
1 Tbsp. butter or margarine
2 tsp. mustard
1/4 onion, finely chopped
    (optional)
1 Tbsp. Worcestershire
    sauce (optional)
salt & pepper lightly

Serves 2

EQUIPMENT

broiler pan
cutting board
measuring spoons
knife

1. Spread first the butter and then the mustard evenly on bread.
2. Form four thin patties from meat (pg. 99), mixing in Worcestershire sauce and onion, if desired.
3. Spread each pattie to edge of each slice of bread.
4. Broil hamburger side up for approximately 7 mins. or until desired doneness.

TERIYAKI BURGER

Oven on broil

Serves 2

INGREDIENTS
1/2 lb. ground beef
2 Tbsp. teriyaki sauce
1/2 tsp. garlic powder
salt & pepper lightly
1 small onion, chopped fine
   (optional)
2 buns, toasted

EQUIPMENT
frying pan
measuring spoons
mixing bowl

1. In mixing bowl, mix (with fingers) ground beef, teriyaki sauce, garlic powder, salt & pepper and onion.
2. Form mixture into 2 patties (see page 99).
3. Broil 4 - 5 inches below flame (see page 100).
4. Can be served on buns or toast. (see page 102 for options).

BURGERS WITH A SECRET

Oven on broil

Serves 2

INGREDIENTS

1/2 lb. ground beef
2 Tbsp. grated cheese
(or a favorite soft cheese, non-grated)
2 med. mushrooms
1 Tbsp. Worcestershire sauce
1 Tbsp. butter or margarine

EQUIPMENT

frying pan
mixing bowl
plate
measuring spoons
grater or knife
knife, large
spatula

1. In bowl, mix ground beef and Worcestershire sauce. Use your fingers, but be gentle!
2. On a plate form 4 very thin patties. Press the patties down with your hand against the plate so that they don't break apart.
3. Grate cheese (or cut into small pieces).
4. Wipe off and finely slice mushrooms, including stems.
5. Melt butter in pan over medium heat.
6. Add mushrooms and saute until soft and golden, about 4 - 5 mins.
7. In center of each pattie, place half each of cheese and mushrooms.
8. Place remaining 2 patties over these (you may want to use the spatula to help handle patties) and pinch edges, sealing completely.
9. Broil 4 - 5 inches below flame (see page 100)

GINGER BEEF

Stove top

Serves 2

INGREDIENTS

1 lb. ground beef
2 medium tomatoes
1 medium onion
1-1/2 tsp. ginger
1 tsp. garlic powder
1 Tbsp. soy sauce
1 Tbsp. cooking oil

EQUIPMENT

frying pan
measuring spoons
spatula
knife

1. Finely chop onion.
2. Heat oil in frying pan over medium flame (about 1 min.)
3. Add onion and saute for 3 - 5 mins. until soft, stirring occasionally.
4. Crumble ground beef into pan and add ginger, garlic, and soy sauce.
5. Cook beef and onion mixture 4 - 5 mins., stirring occasionally,or until beef is browned.
6. Pour off excess oil.
7. Slice tomatoes into wedges and add to pan.
8. Cook another 2 - 3 mins., stirring occasionally.

MEAT & POTATOES

Stove top

Serves 2

INGREDIENTS

3/4 lb. ground beef
2 medium potatoes
1 medium onion
1 Tbsp. butter or margarine
2-1/2 cups water
1 small can corn (optional)
1/2 tsp. salt
1/4 tsp. pepper

EQUIPMENT

medium pot
measuring cup
measuring spoons
large spoon
knife

1. Wash potatoes. Do not peel. Cut into bite-size pieces.
2. Peel and cut onion into bite-size pieces.
3. Melt butter over medium heat in pot. Add onion and fry 4 mins.
4. Crumble meat into pot with onions and continue cooking until meat is browned (approx. 5 mins.) Stir occasionally.
5. Add potatoes to pot and pour in water.
6. Bring to boil, then reduce heat to medium-low.
7. Cook for approx. 20 mins. (add corn after 15 mins.), stirring occasionally, until potatoes are soft.
8. Season to taste with salt & pepper.

BROCCOLI BURGER

Stove top

Serves 2

INGREDIENTS

1/2 lb. ground beef
2 Tbsp. Worcestershire sauce
(or any bottled sauce
you prefer)
1-1/2 cups broccoli, chopped
into bite-size pieces
1 Tbsp. butter or margarine

EQUIPMENT

frying pan
mixing bowl
measuring cup
measuring spoons
knife

1. Melt butter in frying pan over medium heat.
2. Wash and chop broccoli and add to pan. Cook approx.5 -7 mins., stirring frequently, until slightly undercooked. Scoop out of pan and set aside.
3. Crumble ground beef into frying pan over medium heat.
4. Add Worcestershire sauce.
5. Cook, stirring occasionally, 5 - 7 mins. or until meat is almost done.
6. Drain grease from pan.
7. Add broccoli to meat in pan.
8. Cook broccoli and meat together until desired doneness. Broccoli should be slightly crunchy.

SLOPPY JOES

Stove top

Serves 2

INGREDIENTS

1/2 lb. ground beef
3 Tbsp. chili sauce
1/4 cup water
1/4 cup finely chopped onion
   (1/2 medium onion)
1/4 tsp. garlic powder
2 buns or toast or
   English muffins
salt & pepper lightly

EQUIPMENT

frying pan
measuring cup
measuring spoons
knife
large spoon

1. Crumble ground beef into a frying pan over medium heat.
2. Peel and finely chop onion.
3. After 3 mins. of cooking meat, add chopped onions.
4. Cook until done (4 - 7 mins. more).
5. Drain grease from frying pan.
6. Add chili sauce, water, garlic powder, salt & pepper.
7. Mix together well and simmer, uncovered, over low heat about 15 mins. or until thickened enough to spoon over toasted buns.

TACO SALAD

Stove top

Serves 2

INGREDIENTS

1 lb. ground beef
2 cups corn chips (approx.)
1 small pkg. taco seasoning mix
4 leaves of lettuce
1 medium tomato
1 cup Cheddar cheese, grated
　French dressing

EQUIPMENT

frying pan
spatula
measuring cup
knife
grater or large knife
2 dinner plates

1. Crumble ground beef into frying pan and cook over medium flame until browned. Drain off excess fat.
2. Add taco seasonings and cook according to package.
3. Wash and slice lettuce into thin strips.
4. Wash and chop tomato into small pieces.
5. Grate cheese (or cut into fine pieces).
6. Cover 2 plates with corn chips, then layer with ground beef, cheese, lettuce, tomato, more cheese and top with French dressing.

　Ole!

PASTA

THE MOST IMPORTANT PART OF COOKING PASTA IS TIMING; IT MUST NOT BE OVERCOOKED OR UNDERCOOKED. TASTE IT WHILE COOKING. YOUR PASTA SHOULD BE JUST PAST CRUNCHINESS — SOFT ENOUGH TO BE EASILY CUT WITH A FORK.

BREAKING SPAGHETTI STRANDS IN HALF BEFORE COOKING MAKES IT EASIER TO FIT THEM INTO THE POT.

WATER MUST BE BOILING BEFORE PASTA IS ADDED.

ALWAYS ADD 2 TEASPOONS OF COOKING OIL AND 1 TEASPOON OF SALT TO YOUR BOILING WATER TO PREVENT THE PASTA FROM STICKING.

PASTA COOLS QUICKLY, SO IF YOU WANT TO SERVE IT HOT, PLAN YOUR COOKING TIME CAREFULLY ACCORDING TO WHEN YOU WANT TO SIT DOWN FOR YOUR MEAL.

SPAGHETTI CIRCLES

Use the measuring circles below to gauge the correct serving size. Hold one end of a handful of spaghetti against the circle until you have enough pasta to fill in the serving size desired.

BAKED SPAGHETTI

Preheat oven 350°

Serves 2

INGREDIENTS
spaghetti (see page 114)
1 cup spaghetti sauce,
   store-bought
1 Tbsp. margarine or butter
3 tsp. vegetable oil
1 tsp. salt
Parmesan cheese (optional)

EQUIPMENT
large pot
baking pan
small saucepan
measuring cup
measuring spoons
collander
paper towels

1. Fill pot half full of water and add 2 tsp. oil and salt.
2. Bring to boil.
3. Break spaghetti in half and add to boiling water. Keep flame on high, but do not permit the pot to boil over. Stir frequently. Cook 7 - 10 mins.
4. Meanwhile, pour spaghetti sauce in sauce pan and cook over low heat for 5 mins. Set aside.
5. Drain cooked spaghetti in collander. Briefly rinse under HOT water.
6. With paper towel, spread 1 tsp. oil (or 1/2 Tbsp. margarine) evenly on bottom and sides of baking dish.
7. Pour spaghetti into baking dish. Pour over sauce and lightly sprinkle with Parmesan.
8. Cut margarine into small pieces and dot top of dish. Bake uncovered for 15 mins.

SPAGHETTI AGLIO E OLIO (garlic & oil)

Stove top

Serves 2

INGREDIENTS

spaghetti (see page 114)
1/2 tsp. garlic powder
1 Tbsp. margarine or butter
2 tsp. vegetable oil
1 tsp. salt
1/2 tsp. dried basil or fresh
    chopped parsley (optional)
Parmesan cheese (optional)

EQUIPMENT

large pot
measuring spoons
sauce pan
collander

1. Fill large pot half full of water and add oil & salt.
2. Bring to boil.
3. Break spaghetti in half and add to boiling water. Keep flame on high, but do not permit the pot to boil over. Stir frequently.
4. Two mins. before spaghetti is done (after about 5 mins. of cooking), melt margarine in sauce pan over low heat.
5. When margarine is melted, add garlic, stir and remove from heat. If you wish, you may add dried basil or fresh, chopped parsley.
6. Drain cooked spaghetti in collander. Briefly rinse under HOT water and return to pot.
7. Mix melted margarine and garlic into spaghetti. If desired, sprinkle with Parmesan cheese. Serve.

SPAGHETTI CARBONARA

Stove top

Serves 2

INGREDIENTS

spaghetti (see page 114)
3 slices of bacon
1 egg
1 tsp. salt
1 tsp. pepper
2 tsp. vegetable oil
Parmesan cheese (optional)

EQUIPMENT

large pot
frying pan
small bowl
measuring spoons
collander
fork
paper towels

1. Fill large pot half full of water and add oil & salt. Put over high heat.
2. Place bacon strips in frying pan over medium heat, turning occasionally until slightly crispy. Remove from heat.
3. Drain bacon on paper towels and crumble into small pieces after cooled.
4. Break spaghetti in half and add to boiling water. Keep a high flame, but do not permit the pot to boil over. Stir frequently.
5. Drain cooked spaghetti (7 - 10 mins. - taste for desired doneness) in collander and rinse under HOT water. Return spaghetti to pot.
6. Break egg into small bowl and beat with fork until frothy.
7. Add egg and bacon to hot spaghetti and mix thoroughly; the spaghetti will cook the egg! Add pepper & mix.
8. If desired, sprinkle additional Parmesan cheese overall.

FETTUCINE

Stove top

INGREDIENTS

1-1/2 cups flat medium noodles
(spaghetti may be substituted)
1/2 cup heavy cream
1/4 cup margarine or butter
1/2 cup grated Parmesan
cheese.
1 tsp. salt
2 tsp. vegetable oil
pepper to taste

Serves 2

EQUIPMENT

large pot
sauce pan
measuring cup
measuring spoons
collander
large spoon

1. Fill large pot half full of water, add oil & salt; bring to boil.
2. Add noodles to boiling water. Keep heat on high, but do not permit the pot to boil over. Stir frequently.
3. While noodles are cooking, melt margarine in cream over low heat in sauce pan.
4. Remove from heat when margarine is completely melted.
5. Add cheese to sauce, pepper lightly, and stir until mixture is well blended.
6. Drain cooked noodles (7 - 10 mins.) in collander and rinse briefly under HOT water.
7. Return to pot.
8. Pour sauce over noodles, mix well and serve.
9. If desired, sprinkle additional Parmesan over each serving.

CREAMY MACARONI

Preheat oven 400°

Serves 2

INGREDIENTS

1-1/2 cups macaroni
   (or spaghetti)
2 Tbsp. margarine or butter
1/2 cup sour cream (4 ozs.)
2 tsp. vegetable oil
grated Parmesan cheese, to
   taste
1 tsp. salt
bread crumbs (optional)
   sprinkled lightly

EQUIPMENT

large pot
baking pan
measuring cup
measuring spoons
collander
paper towels

1. Fill pot half full of water and add oil & salt; bring to boil.
2. Add macaroni to pot. Keep heat on high, but do not permit the pot to boil over. Stir frequently.
3. After 7 - 10 mins., drain macaroni in collander and rinse under HOT water. Return to pot.
4. Add margarine to pot, stirring until melted.
5. Add sour cream to pot; mix thoroughly.
6. With paper towel spread 1 tsp. oil on bottom and sides of baking pan.
7. Pour macaroni into pan.
8. Sprinkle enough cheese to cover. (Sprinkle with bread crumbs.)
9. Bake 10 - 15 mins. or until top is browned.

PASTA SALAD

Stove top

Serves 2

INGREDIENTS

1 cup pasta (curls, shells, etc.)
1 carrot
1 stalk celery
1/4 cup vegetable oil
2 tsp. vegetable oil (separate
from above)
1/8 cup vinegar
1 tsp. basil
1 tsp. salt
salt to taste

EQUIPMENT

large pot
small saucepan
measuring cup
measuring spoons
knife
collander

1. Fill both pots half full of water. Add 2 tsp.oil & 1 tsp. salt to large one.
2. Bring to boil and add pasta to large pot. Cook 7 - 10 mins.
3. Meanwhile, wash carrot. Cut off leafy end. Slice into 1/4" rounds.
4. Wash celery & cut into bite-size pieces.
5. Place carrot and celery in small saucepan and boil for 2 mins.
6. Rinse vegetables under COOL water in collander for 1 minute, drain and set aside.
7. Drain cooked pasta and rinse under COOL water for 1 min.
8. Place pasta, carrot & celery in bowl. Add oil, vinegar and basil and mix well. Season with salt.

LASAGNA

Preheat oven 350°   Serves 2 for 4 meals

Before deciding that this recipe is too difficult (it isn't) or takes too long (it doesn't), we want you to weigh two factors: Half an hour of cooking vs. 8 ready-made meals - that's how many servings you'll get.

Think about it. Half an hour of mild slavery and you can have 8 delicious dinners that you can freeze and cook weeks later in 15 minutes.

Decide? Good. Start cookin'.

INGREDIENTS
1 lb. box lasagna noodles
2 lb. jar spaghetti sauce, store-bought
1 lb. ground beef
1 lb. Ricotta cheese
1 lb. Mozzarella cheese
1 tsp. salt
2 tsp. vegetable oil
salt & pepper to taste

EQUIPMENT
large pot
frying pan
large baking pan
grater or large knife
measuring spoons
collander
spatula
spoon

(continued)

LASAGNA (con't.)

1. Crumble ground beef into frying pan over medium heat.
2. Cook until meat is browned (about 5 mins.). Drain.
3. Pour 3/4 of jar of spaghetti sauce into pan with meat and simmer uncovered for 20 mins., stirring occasionally. (Let simmer while you prepare rest of dish.)
4. Fill large pot half full of water and add salt & oil.
5. Bring to boil.
6. Add noodles (about 18) one at a time to boiling water. Stir occasionally & gently, not permitting noodles to stick to bottom of pot or to each other. Cook about 12 mins. - taste for desired doneness.
7. While noodles are cooking, grate or slice Mozzarella into very fine pieces.
8. Drain noodles. Rinse under COLD water just enough so that you can handle noodles without burning your fingers.
9. Turn off heat beneath sauce. Open Ricotta and place teaspoon nearby. Now, you're ready for the fun part!
10. In baking pan, layer noodles (lengthwise, slightly over-lapping), sauce, both cheeses (Ricotta is spooned about every 2 inches), salt & pepper lightly, in that order. You'll probably be making 4 layers, so think of your ingredients in quarters. End with cheese on top.
11. Bake 15 mins.. Serve hot. Cut remaining portion, when cooled, into squares approx. 3 inches square. Freeze separately for future meals.
12. REHEATING: If defrosted: Bake 15 mins. at 350° wrapped in tin foil. If frozen: Bake 30 mins. at 350° wrapped in tin foil.

HONESTLY NOW, AREN'T YOU HAVING FUN ?!

EGGS

NO, THEY'RE NOT JUST FOR BREAKFAST! LET'S LOOK AT THE GOOD AND BAD POINTS ABOUT EGGS —

FIRST, THE GOOD :

1. INEXPENSIVE
2. FILLING
3. VERSATILE - CAN BE COOKED WITH MANY ADDITIONS.
4. EASY TO PREPARE AND COOK.
5. NEVER NEED DEFROSTING

NOW THE BAD...

WE COULDN'T THINK OF ANY!

SCRAMBLED EGGS WITH ONION

Stove top

Serves 2

INGREDIENTS

1 medium yellow skinned onion
6 eggs
1 Tbsp. margarine or butter
1/4 tsp. salt
1 Tbsp. milk or water
1/2 tsp. paprika
pepper to taste

EQUIPMENT

mixing bowl
frying pan
measuring spoons
knife
fork

1. Peel onion under running water to prevent tears. Chop into small pieces.
2. Break eggs into bowl.
3. Add paprika, salt & milk.
4. Beat with fork until frothy, well-blended, and set aside.
5. Melt the margarine in frying pan over medium heat.
6. Add the onions to the pan and saute until soft, stirring occasionally. (about 5 mins.)
7. When onions are soft and slightly yellow, add the eggs.
8. As the eggs begin to thicken, about 1 minute, stir with fork making sure to scrape bottom of pan.
9. When most of the liquid has thickened, taste the eggs so that you can decide how well done you prefer.
10. Serve immediately.

SCRAMBLED EGGS WITH VEGETABLES

The following vegetables can be substituted for onion in the preceding recipe.

Vegetables must be washed and finely chopped (about 1/2 cup). See page 150-152 for further instructions on washing and preparing vegetables.

Next to each vegetable below is the approximate cooking time before adding the eggs:

BEAN SPROUTS 1 - 2 mins.

BROCCOLI 3 - 4 mins.

CAULIFLOWER 3 - 4 mins.

CELERY 3 - 4 mins.

EGGPLANT 2 - 3 mins.

BELL PEPPER 3 - 4 mins.

MUSHROOMS 2 - 3 mins.

PARSLEY 1 - 2 mins.

SPINACH 1 - 2 mins.

ZUCCHINI 3- 4 mins.

Grated cheese (about 2/3 cup) and 1 medium tomato, chopped, can be added at the same time as eggs.

BASIC OMELETTE

Stove top

INGREDIENTS
6 eggs
1/2 Tbsp. milk or water
1/4 tsp. salt
1 Tbsp. margarine or butter

Serves 2

EQUIPMENT
frying pan with lid
mixing bowl
measuring spoons
spatula
fork

1. In bowl, combine eggs, milk & salt and beat with fork until frothy.
2. Melt margarine in frying pan over medium heat.
3. Pour in eggs and cover pan for 3 mins.
4. Then, you must tilt the pan slightly and, with spatula, gently lift edge of your omelette to permit the uncooked eggs to run beneath. Repeat this procedure until all of the eggs are cooked.
5. Now, slip spatula beneath one half of the omelette and gently fold it over itself, forming a half circle.
6. Slip onto plate, cut in half and serve.

SEE PAGE 129 FOR VARIATIONS

OMELETTE VARIATIONS

General note: you need two pans - One for preparing eggs, and One for preparing omelette filling.

1. VEGETABLES - 1/2 cup chopped.

> Prepare vegetables by sauteing as described on pages 150-152 before you begin preparing eggs. Put aside. Add to omelette after cooking for at least 2 mins.

Suggestions:	
celery	tomato
mushroom	zucchini
bell pepper	avocado
onion	bean sprouts
	parsley

2. CHEESE - 1/2 cup grated or 4 slices

> Add to omelette in last 30 seconds of cooking.

Suggestions:	
Monterey Jack	
Swiss	Jarlsberg
Cheddar	Parmesan
Mozzarella	Muenster

(continued)

OMELETTE VARIATIONS (Con't.)

3. BACON - 3 strips
    Fry in pan over medium heat until crispy. Paper towel dry. Break into small pieces. Add to omelette in last 30 seconds of cooking.

4. LUNCHEON MEAT - 3 slices, chopped
    Add to omelette in last 30 seconds of cooking.

5. SOUR CREAM - 3 tablespoons
    Add just before folding omelette.

6. COTTAGE CHEESE - 3 tablespoons
    Add just before folding omelette.

7. JELLY - 2 tablespoons
    Add just before folding omelette.

CURRIED CREAMED EGGS

Stove top

Serves 2

INGREDIENTS

4 eggs
1/2 tsp. curry powder
1-1/4 cups milk
2 Tbsp. flour
2 Tbsp. margarine or butter
1/4 tsp. salt
toast or English muffin

EQUIPMENT

2 saucepans
measuring cup
measuring spoons
large spoon
knife

1. In one saucepan, cover unbroken eggs with water and boil for 7 mins.
2. While eggs are boiling, melt butter in other saucepan over low heat.
3. Stir flour and salt into melted butter until creamy.
4. Slowly add milk to mixture, stirring constantly, until sauce is thick and smooth. Do not permit to boil. Continue cooking over low heat for at least 10 mins., stir occassionally.
5. When eggs are done, rinse them thoroughly in cold water and gently peel off shells.
6. Slice eggs.
7. Mix curry into sauce. Gently fold in eggs and cook 5 mins., stirring ocassionally.
8. Serve over toast or toasted English muffins (especially good over raisin English muffins).

EGGS 'N APPLES 'N DOGS

Stove top

Serves 2

INGREDIENTS

3 eggs
1 medium apple
2 hot dogs
1 medium onion
1 Tbsp. butter or margarine
1/4 tsp. salt

EQUIPMENT

frying pan
mixing bowl
knife
fork

1. Cut apple in half and cut out core. Peel onion.
2. Chop apple, onion and hot dogs into small pieces.
3. Melt butter in frying pan over medium heat.
4. Add onions and saute until soft (about 2 mins.).
5. Add hot dogs and apples to onions and continue cooking for another 4-5 mins., stirring occasionally.
6. Break eggs into bowl and beat with fork until frothy.
7. When apples begin to soften, add eggs and stir constantly.
8. Cook until eggs thicken, according to desired doneness.

EGGS BENNIE

An informal version of Eggs Benedict.
Stove top

Serves 2

INGREDIENTS

4 eggs
4 slices of English muffins
4 slices of bacon
2 Tbsp. butter or margarine
4 slices of firm cheese

EQUIPMENT

2 frying pans
spatula
measuring spoons
fork
paper towels

1. Toast English muffins under broiler or in toaster.
2. In pan over med. heat, cook bacon until crispy. Break into small pieces.
3. Melt butter in other pan over low heat.
4. Being careful not to break the yolks, add eggs to pan with butter and cook over low heat until the whites are firm (You may like your yolks soft or hard, so continue cooking until your desired doneness.).
5. Sprinkle crumpled bacon over English muffins. Slip eggs over bacon and place 1 slice of cheese over each.
6. Place under broiler until cheese is melted (about 30 seconds).

SEAFOOD

THE MOST IMPORTANT RULE FOR COOKING SEAFOOD:

DON'T OVERCOOK

FILLETS:

- A FILLET IS THE SIDE OF A FISH CUT AWAY FROM THE BACKBONE AND IS ALMOST BONELESS.

- FIGURE ON ABOUT ½ POUND PER SERVING.

- FROZEN FISH FILLETS ARE USUALLY MORE AVAILABLE AND LESS EXPENSIVE THAN FRESH FISH.

FRESH FISH:

LEAST EXPENSIVE	MOST EXPENSIVE
FILLET OF SOLE	SALMON
FLOUNDER	HALIBUT
TURBOT	TROUT
PERCH	
COD	

<u>LEAST EXPENSIVE</u> (CONT.)

HADDOCK
RED SNAPPER

STORE FRESH FISH NO MORE THAN 2 DAYS IN THE REFRIGERATOR.

AFTER COOKING, FISH CAN BE REFRIGERATED IN A COVERED CONTAINER NO LONGER THAN 3 DAYS, AND FROZEN NO MORE THAN 3 MONTHS.

THAWING INSTRUCTIONS

Do not thaw fresh fish at room temperature - thaw overnight in refrigerator.

If thawing must be speeded up, immerse fish in waterproof package in cool water.

Use immediately after thawing.

Dry with paper towel before cooking.

Frozen breaded fish fillets or stick should not be thawed. Cook directly from freezer. If they do thaw, cook immediately; do not refreeze.

Try to buy only boneless fresh fish. The extra expense is worth the ease of preparation.

SEAFOOD

BROILED FISH ITALIANO

Oven on Broil

Serves 2

INGREDIENTS
1 lb. boneless fillet of fish
(haddock, cod, etc.)
bottled Italian dressing
2 tsp. butter or margarine
salt & pepper lightly
1 Tbsp. lemon juice (optional)
paprika (optional)
1 tsp. soy sauce (optional)
1/2 tsp. garlic powder
(optional)

EQUIPMENT
broiler pan
measuring spoons
bowl

1. Immerse defrosted fish in just enough Italian dressing to completely cover for 15 mins.
2. Remove fish from dressing and place on broiler pan. Dot with butter.
3. Salt & pepper lightly.
4. Broil under flame 5 - 8 mins. (depending upon thickness) or until fish flakes apart easily.
5. When fish is just about done, sprinkle paprika lightly and evenly and return to broiler for 30 seconds.
OPTIONAL: Instead of marinating fish in dressing, sprinkle lemon juice or soy sauce or garlic powder over fillet just before cooking.
All three are good together, too.

SHRIMP SALAD

Wonderful for hot evenings!
Stove top

Serves 2

INGREDIENTS

1/2 lb. small cooked shrimp
1 medium cucumber
1 egg (hard boiled)
1/3 cup mayonnaise
1 tsp. mustard
1 tsp. lemon juice
1/2 tsp. dill
1/8 tsp. pepper
4 leaves lettuce
1 tomato

EQUIPMENT

sauce pan
bowl
measuring cup
measuring spoons
knife
mixing spoon
peeler
2 dinner plates

1. Place unbroken egg in pan of boiling water for 7 mins.
2. Meanwhile, mix together in bowl: mayonnaise, mustard, lemon juice, dill and pepper.
3. Peel and chop cucumber into small pieces.
4. Rinse egg under cold water. Peel and slice.
5. Add cucumber, egg and shrimp to mayonnaise mixture and blend gently.
6. Wash lettuce and tear into bite-size pieces and sprinkle over plates.
7. Wash & cut tomatoes into bite-size pieces and place evenly over lettuce.
8. Spoon equal portions of shrimp salad into center of plates and serve.

TUNA BOAT

Cold

Serves 2

INGREDIENTS

1 can, 9-1/2 oz., tuna, drained
1/2 cup mayonnaise
4 Tbsp. relish (sweet pickle)
1 tomato, sliced 1/4 inch thick
1 avocado
1 stalk celery, chopped, optional
1/4 onion, chopped, optional
1 hard boiled egg, optional

EQUIPMENT

mixing bowl
measuring cup
measuring spoons
large spoon
can opener
knife

1. Cut avocado in half lengthwise. Cut all the way to the pit & all the way around.
2. Chop the blade into the pit, twist and remove.
3. With spoon carefully scoop as one piece the avocado halves out of skins.
4. Mix tuna, mayonnaise, relish & any optional ingredient together.
5. Chop tomato and mix into tuna.
6. Spoon into avocado halves and serve.

Serving suggestions for tuna mixture:
    A. On toasted English Muffin, topped with any firm cheese & broiled until cheese melts.
    B. On toasted Hamburger buns.

BOUILLABAISE

Don't let anyone con you - Bouillabaise is Fish Stew. Simplified, it is absolutely delicious.

Stove top

Serves 2 for 2 meals

INGREDIENTS

1 lb. boneless fish fillet
   (haddock, perch or cod or
   mixture)
1 can, 28 oz. concentrated
   cooked tomatoes
1 med. onion
1/2 cup celery, chopped
4 tbsp. butter or margarine
1/2 tsp. basil
1/2 tsp. Worcestershire sauce
salt to taste.

EQUIPMENT

large pot
measuring spoons
measuring cup
large spoon
knife
can opener

1. Cut fish into bite-size pieces.
2. Peel & chop onion into small pieces.
3. Wash & chop celery into small pieces.
3. In pot, melt butter over medium heat.
4. Add onions and celery and cook until soft.
5. Add rest of ingredients, stir together and cook uncovered for 45 mins. over low heat until fish
   is thoroughly cooked.
6. Store leftovers covered in refrigerator. Reheat in saucepan over medium heat for 15 mins.

FISH & DIP

Preheat oven 350°

INGREDIENTS

1 lb. boneless fish fillet
(haddock, cod, etc.)
1/4 cup heavy cream
1/4 cup seasoned bread
    crumbs

Serves 2

EQUIPMENT

baking pan
2 shallow bowls
measuring cup
paper towels

1. Pour cream in one bowl and bread crumbs in the other.
2. Wash fillet and paper towel dry.
3. Dip fillet in cream, coating completely.
4. Dip in bread crumbs, coating evenly. Place in baking dish.
5. Bake 20 mins. or until fish easily flakes apart. Do not overbake.

FISH DRESSED IN WHITE

Preheat oven 350°

Serves 2

INGREDIENTS

1 lb. boneless fillet of fish
  (haddock, cod, etc.)
1/4 cup sour cream
1/4 tsp. paprika
1/4 tsp. salt
1 tsp. parsley, chopped fine

EQUIPMENT

baking pan
measuring cup
measuring spoons
paper towels
knife

1. Wash fillet and paper towel dry.
2. Rub fillet with paprika and salt.
3. Place in baking pan and spoon sour cream over fish.
4. Bake 20 mins. or until fish flakes apart easily.
5. Sprinkle parsley over fillet before serving.

FISH IN MUSTARD SAUCE

Stove top

Serves 2

INGREDIENTS

1 lb. boneless fish fillet
(haddock, cod, etc.)
3 Tbsp. mustard
1 Tbsp. margarine or butter
1 egg
1/2 cup heavy cream
1/2 Tbsp. vinegar
1/4 tsp. dill

EQUIPMENT

frying pan
saucepan
measuring cup
measuring spoons
large spoon
spatula
paper towels

1. Wash fillet and paper towel dry.
2. Melt margarine in frying pan over medium heat.
3. Place fish in melted butter and fry over low heat until done, turning once. 5 - 10 mins., depending upon thickness of fish.
4. Meanwhile, mix all other ingredients in saucepan and stir over low heat, until mixture begins to thicken.
5. Pour over fish and serve.

SALMON CROQUETTES

Stove top

Serves 2

INGREDIENTS

1 can, 15-1/2 oz., red salmon
1/2 cup seasoned bread
   crumbs
2 Tbsp. fresh chopped parsley
2 Tbsp. onion, chopped
1/4 cup milk
1 egg
1 Tbsp. lemon juice
1 Tbsp. vegetable oil
1 Tbsp. margarine or butter

EQUIPMENT

frying pan
2 mixing bowls
measuring cup
measuring spoons
spatula
knife
can opener
fork

1. Drain salmon; place in bowl and remove any skin and bones.
2. Peel and finely chop onion.
3. Wash and finely chop parsley.
4. Mix salmon, bread crumbs, onion, and lemon juice in bowl.
5. Beat together egg and milk in small bowl until well blended. Add to salmon mixture and blend well.
6. With hands, form salmon into four 1/2-inch-thick patties.
7. Heat oil & margarine in pan over medium flame for 2 mins.
8. Place patties in pan and fry 4 - 5 mins. per side, until golden brown.

VEGETABLES

THE FOLLOWING PAGES DESCRIBE THE MOST BASIC VEGETABLE COOKING AND PREPARING METHODS. YOU NEED ONLY USE THEM AND YOUR SIDE DISHES WILL BE PERFECT EVERY TIME. THE STEPS ARE SIMPLE:

1. DECIDE WHICH VEGETABLE YOU ARE GOING TO COOK.

2. LOOK IT UP ON THE PREP & COOK CHART, P. 99-101.

3. CHOOSE YOUR COOKING METHOD AND REFER TO THE COOKING VEGETABLES DESCRIPTIONS, P. 98.

4. FINALLY, FOR SEASONING, READ EXPERIMENTAL CORNER, P. 102-103.

— ON THE WEEKLY SCHEDULES, WE HAVE SUGGESTED SOME VEGETABLE PREPARATIONS... FEEL FREE TO VARY THEM.

FROZEN VS. CANNED:

OF COURSE, FRESH IS ALWAYS OUR FIRST CHOICE, BUT IF YOU WANT A VEGETABLE TOWARD THE END OF THE WEEK,

YOU'LL HAVE TO SETTLE FOR FROZEN OR CANNED. MOST FRESH VEGETABLES WILL LAST ONLY 3-4 DAYS IN YOUR REFRIGERATOR. BESIDES, IT WILL BE NICE TO TAKE A NIGHT OFF ONCE IN A WHILE TO SIMPLY POP A PREPARED VEGETABLE INTO A POT.

OUR ONLY COMMENT IS THAT FROZEN USUALLY TASTES CLOSER TO FRESH THAN CANNED.

IF YOU HAVE ANY QUESTIONS ABOUT SIZE OR RIPENESS, ASK THE PRODUCE MANAGER OF YOUR STORE FOR HELP.

COOKING METHODS

You don't have to peel most vegetables; just wash them thoroughly. MOST IMPORTANT: Most green vegetables are done when they can be easily pierced with a knife. DO NOT OVERCOOK.
There are 4 basic cooking methods:

1. STEAMING:

Our favorite because it keeps most of the vitamins & nutrients in the vegetable and it is the fastest & easiest method. A steamer is a collapsible metal basket. (They sell for approx. $5.00) Place the steamer in your pot & fill with 1 - 2 inches of water. Bring water to boil & add vegetable. Cover pot with lid and reduce heat to medium. BEWARE: some vegetables will need more water added before they are done. Don't let your pot boil empty.

2. BOILING:

Fill pot 3/4 full of water. Bring to boil. Add vegetable.
Test frequently: do not overcook.

3. SAUTEING:

In medium frying pan heat 1 Tbsp.butter. Add vegetable and cook over medium heat, stirring frequently. Vegetables should be cut into small pieces. With eggplant or dense vegetables like carrots you may need to add a few drops of water to the pan & cover with a lid for a few minutes to help soften them.

4. BAKING:

Simply place vegetable, wrapped in tin foil, in preheated oven at designated temperature.

PREP & COOK CHART

Vegetable & Season Available	Preparation	Size	Steam	Boil	Saute	Bake
				(in minutes)		
Artichoke Sept.–May	Cut off stem. Wash well. If desired, cut 1/3 off top.	Med.	25-35	20-40	N/A	N/A
Asparagus Feb.–June	Snap off tough white ends.	whole: cut up:	10-15 6-9	5-8 3-4	N/A 10-15	N/A
Green Beans All year	Cut off tips. Slice diagonally.	whole: cut up:	10-15 8-13	5-10 4-7	N/A 5-7	N/A
Broccoli All year	Remove large outer leaves. Cut off tough ends of stalk.	whole: cut up:	10-15 8-13	5-10 3-7	N/A 5-7	N/A
Brussel Sprouts Sept-March	Remove wilted outer leaves. Cut 1/4" deep into stem.	whole:	15-20	5-7	N/A	N/A
Cabbage All year	Remove wilted outer leaves.	quartrd: shred'd:	25-35 10-15	10-15 5-7	3-5 3-5	N/A
Carrot All year	Cut off stem & tip. Peel, if desired. If not, wash.	whole: cut up:	20-30 10-20	15-20 5-15	N/A 7-10	N/A
Cauliflower All year	Cut off stem & leaves. Break into large flowerets.	whole: cut up:	10-15 8-13	10-15 5-10	N/A 7-10	N/A
Celery All year	Separate stalks. Cut off leaves & white part of base.	whole: cut up:	15-20 10-15	12-15 10-13	5-6 4-5	N/A

PREP & COOK CHART

Vegetable & Season Available	Preparation	Size	Steam	Boil	Saute	Bake
				(in minutes)		
Corn on the cob May–Dec.	Remove husks & silk. Boil in unsalted water.	whole:	15-20	3-5	N/A	N/A
Eggplant All year	Cut off stem. Peel before or after cooking.	cut up:	15-20	5-10	5-10	N/A
Mushroom All year	Wipe clean. Do not immerse in water. Cut off end of stem	whole: cut up:	N/A N/A	N/A N/A	N/A 4-5	N/A N/A
Onion All year	Peel under cool, running water to prevent tears.	whole: cut up:	25-30 20-25	15-20 10-15	N/A 4-5	N/A
Pepper, green Bell Apr.-Dec.	Cut in half. Cut out core. Scoop out seeds.	halves: cut up:	10-15 8-10	6-7 4-5	N/A 4-5	N/A
Potato, Baking All year	Do not peel but wash well. Cut into lg. pcs. for boiling	whole: cut up:	N/A 35-40	N/A 10-15	N/A N/A	1 hr. 400°

PREP & COOK CHART

Vegetable & Season Available	Preparation	Size	Steam	Boil	Saute	Bake
				(in minutes)		
Potato, Sweet All year	Do not peel but wash well.	whole: cut up:	N/A N/A	25-30 20-25	N/A N/A	1 hr. 400°
Snow peas May-Sept.	Cut off tips.	whole:	5-7	1-2	4-6	N/A
Spinach	Wash well; tends to be sandy. Dry. Pinch off stems	whole: leaves:	5-10	1-2	1-2	N/A
Squash, Summer* All year	Cut off stem & tip. Do not peel.	whole: cut up:	10-12	5-10	N/A	20-50 350°
Squash, winter** Oct.-Feb.	Cut in half, scoop out seeds. If baking, cover in tin foil.	halves:	25-35	10-15	N/A	30-90 350°
Tomato All year	Cut out core.	whole: sliced:	2-3 1-2	1-2 1/2-1	N/A 1-1/2	5-10 3-7

*zucchini, yellow crookneck, yellow straightneck, pattypan, scalloped, white cymling.
**acorn, butternut, banana, buttercup, hubbard, pumpkin, spaghetti squash, chayote.

EXPERIMENTAL CORNER

The following are some of the seasonings for vegetables:

Now, come back here! Cooking with herbs or spices is nothing to be frightened about. Your vegetables are not going to emerge tasting like gunpowder. The answer to all your fears is contained in one word:

MODERATION

This book was written to help you start cooking with organization & simplicity. We're not asking you to memorize hundreds of esoteric spices. We feel that, if you went to the trouble to prepare a main entree then you won't want to bother with sauces for a vegetable. That's why we have kept the seasonings simple, basic, yet delicious. Our favorites are these:

Butter (or margarine) - can't beat it; goes with practically everything.

Lemon juice - use very little; especially good on avocado, broccoli, brussels sprouts, carrot, cauliflower & squash.

Garlic powder - use sparingly; good on green beans, mushrooms & asparagus.

EXPERIMENTAL CORNER (Cont.)

Dillweed (dried)   - extremely versatile herb; good on broccoli, brussels sprouts, cauliflower, tomato.

Basil (dried)   - great on veggies, chicken, tomato sauce.
See Fried tomatoes, p. 155.

Oil & vinegar   - 2 parts oil & 1 part vinegar; add a little basil and you have a great vegetable dressing.

Those are the basics. Remember, Moderation. Try a little seasoning - taste the veggie - good? - try a little more - taste - better? - a little more getting to be too much? - so, stop and you've just learned for next time how much of that particular seasoning you prefer. Go for it!

FRIED TOMATOES

Stove top

INGREDIENTS

2 tomatoes
1 Tbsp. butter or margarine
dill or basil, sprinkled lightly
salt, sprinkled lightly

Serves 2

EQUIPMENT

frying pan
knife
measuring spoons
spatula

1. Wash and slice tomatoes 1/2 inch thick.
2. Melt butter in frying pan over medium heat.
3. Add tomato slices to pan.
4. Sprinkle dill or basil and salt.
5. Saute on each side for 1 minute only - Do not overcook.
6. Serve immediately.

EGGPLANT PIZZA

Oven on Broil

Serves 2

INGREDIENTS

1   medium eggplant
1/4   cup vegetable oil
6-8   Tbsp. spaghetti sauce
1/2   lb. Mozzarella cheese
salt lightly

EQUIPMENT

broiling pan
measuring cup
measuring spoons
knife
spoon
spatula

1. Peel eggplant with knife.
2. Cut into 8 slices 1/2 inch thick.
3. Slice cheese thinly.
4. Spoon and thinly spread oil on 1 side of each slice of eggplant.
5. Broil eggplant under flame, oil side up, for 7-8 mins. or until golden brown.
6. Flip eggplant and repeat step 4 - broil only 4-5 mins.
7. Remove eggplant from oven and salt lightly.
8. Spoon enough sauce to cover eggplant and place cheese in thin layer to cover sauce.
9. Broil until cheese bubbles (about 30 seconds).

FRIED ZUCCHINI CIRCLES

Stove top

Serves 2

INGREDIENTS

2 medium zucchini
1 egg
1 Tbsp. milk
1/2 cup flour or bread crumbs
1 Tbsp. cooking oil
1 Tbsp. butter or margarine.
salt & pepper to taste.

EQUIPMENT

frying pan, large
bowl
measuring cup
measuring spoons
spatula
knife
2 plates

1. Wash zucchini under cool water and cut off ends.
2. Slice zucchini into 1/4" thick circles.
3. Pour flour onto 1 plate.
4. Beat egg and milk in bowl until well-blended.
5. Dip slices of zucchini in egg and then in flour, coating both sides. Place on other plate.
6. Heat oil and butter in pan over medium heat. Oil must be very hot. Test by placing one zucchini circle in oil and wait for it to sizzle before adding rest.
7. Gently place zucchini in pan and saute until golden brown on each side. (About 3 - 4 mins. per side). Sprinkle salt & pepper to taste.
8. Allow to cool slightly before serving.

CHEESY-TOMATO

Preheat Oven 350°

Serves 2

INGREDIENTS

4 tomatoes
1 cup grated Cheddar cheese
1 cup croutons
1 medium onion
1 Tbsp. butter or margarine
1 tsp. sugar
1/2 tsp. basil
1/4 tsp. salt

EQUIPMENT

baking pan
measuring cup
measuring spoons
grater
knife

1. Wash and coarsely chop tomatoes. Place evenly in pan.
2. Top tomatoes with croutons.
3. Peel and slice onion thinly and place over croutons.
4. Sprinkle sugar, basil & salt over all.
5. Cover with cheese.
6. Dot top with butter.
7. Bake 30 mins.

PARSLIED CARROTS

Stove top

Serves 2

INGREDIENTS
2 carrots
1-1/2 Tbsp. butter
1/4 cup freshly chopped
        parsley
salt to taste

EQUIPMENT
frying pan
measuring cup
measuring spoons
spatula
knife

1. Wash carrots well. Peel, if you wish, but it is not necessary. Cut off tops.
2. Cut into 1/4 inch rounds.
3. Melt butter in pan over medium heat.
4. Add carrots to pan and cook for 7 mins, turning frequently.
5. Add parsley & salt and cook for 2 more mins.

STUFFED SHIRT POTATOES

Preheat oven 375°

Serves 2

INGREDIENTS

1   large baking potato
1   Tbsp. butter or margarine
4   Tbsp. sour cream
1/2 tsp. basil
paprika, sprinkled lightly
salt & pepper to taste

EQUIPMENT

broiling pan
bowl
measuring spoons
knife
fork
spoon

1. Wash potato (do not peel) and cut in half lengthwise. Wrap each half separately in tin foil.
2. Place halves in oven and bake for 55 mins. until soft.
3. Gently spoon potato out of skins into bowl. Set skins aside.
4. Add butter, sour cream, basil, salt & pepper to potatoes & mix together well with fork (mashing potatoes in the process).
5. Spoon equal quantities of mixture back into skins.
6. Sprinkle lightly with paprika and place under broiler for 3-4 mins. or until slightly browned on top.

VARIATION: Use 1/3 cup grated cheese and 1/2 tsp. dill instead of sour cream and basil.

POTATO SIMPLICITY

There is no need to buy "instant" potato anything. Preparing from scratch is practically just as instant. One potato = one serving.

Fried

Wash potato. Slice thinly.Heat 2 Tbsp. oil in frying pan. Add potato slices to oil and fry until golden (about 7 mins.), turning once. Drain on paper towels.

Mashed

Wash potato. Peel only if desired. Cut into quarters. Fill pot half full of water and bring to boil. Add potatoes to pot and boil until softened (about 20 mins.) Drain in collander. Scoop potatoes into bowl. Add 1 Tbsp. milk (more if you wish creamier potatoes), 2 Tbsp. butter or margarine, salt & pepper to taste and mash with fork until creamy.

Boiled

Wash potato. Fill pot half full of water and bring to boil. Add potatoes and boil until easily pierced with fork (about 20 mins.) Serve with butter and sour cream, if desired. Salt & pepper to taste.

Baked

Wash potato. Wrap in tin foil. Place in oven at 375 for 55 mins. or until easily pierced with fork. Serve with butter & sour cream, if desired. Salt & pepper to taste.

TOSSED SALAD etc.

SALAD SUGGESTIONS

1. WASH AND DRY (WITH PAPER TOWELS) ALL LETTUCES TO KEEP THE LEAVES CRISP AND YOUR DRESSING FROM GETTING WATERY.

2. DON'T CUT LETTUCE WITH A KNIFE - TEAR IT WITH YOUR FINGERS (METAL KNIVES GIVE THE LEAVES A METALLIC TASTE).

3. EXPERIMENT WHEN YOU MAKE A SALAD... YOU'LL BE SURPRISED WHAT YOU CAN MIX TOGETHER AND ENJOY!

BASIC MIXED GREEN SALAD

In the supermarket you'll find a large variety of lettuces. We feel GREENLEAF LETTUCE or RUBY LETTUCE gives the most value for your money. Try the different kinds and decide for yourself.

INGREDIENTS
lettuce
dressing (see pgs. 171 & 172,
or store bought)
OPTIONAL:
croutons
bacon bits
sunflower seeds
bean sprouts
crab meat
tuna fish
hard boiled eggs - chopped olives
cheese (cottage, feta, any
firm cheese)
any vegetable you enjoy raw
shrimp

EQUIPMENT
large bowl
collander
knife
2 forks

1. Wash lettuce thoroughly and drain in collander.
2. Wash and chop any additional vegetable you choose into bite-size pieces.
3. Place lettuce and other vegetables into bowl, adding any other optional ingredients you prefer.
4. Mix lightly with your choice of dressing.
5. Sprinkle top with croutons or bacon bits, if desired.

AVOCADO/PAPAYA SALAD

Want a double aphrodisiac? Watch out for this one!

Cold

Serves 2

INGREDIENTS
1 ripe avocado
1 ripe papaya
1/4 cup vegetable oil
1 Tbsp. lemon juice
salt to taste

EQUIPMENT
bowl
measuring cup
measuring spoons
knife
spoon

1. Cut avocado in half lengthwise. Cut all the way to the pit & all the way around.
2. Chop the blade into the pit, twist and remove.
3. With spoon carefully scoop whole avocado halves out of skins.
4. Slice thinly, being careful to keep the avocado slices lying together to keep the basic shape.
5. Cut papaya in half lengthwise. Scoop out all seeds.
6. Scoop papaya out of skin and slice as you did the avocado.
7. Arrange avocado and papaya on plate (interchanging every other slice, if you have the patience).
8. Sprinkle oil, lemon juice and salt over all.
9. Eat with a very good friend.

FRUIT SALAD

Want something light and tasty as you sweat on a hot Saturday afternoon? Even if it's not afternoon? Even if you're not sweating? Try a luscious fruit salad.

The thing about fruit salad is that you have to be flexible; you have to go with what is available in the present season. Our recommendation is to see what looks best in the market and use your imagination. All the equipment you need is a bowl, a knife, and a serving spoon.

WINTER FRUITS
apple
orange
banana
pinapple
grapefruit
pear
tangerine

SUMMER FRUITS
peach   blueberry
apricot   boysenberry
plum   strawberry
melon   cherry
grape   nectarine

Fruit salad can be a bowl of one kind of fruit chopped into bite-size pieces or it can be a bountiful mixture of everyting in season - it's up to you! Have fun!

COLE SLAW

Cold

Serves 2

INGREDIENTS

1/2 head cabbage
1/4 cup mayonnaise
1   Tbsp. vinegar
2   Tbsp. sugar
1/4 tsp. salt
1/4 tsp. garlic powder

EQUIPMENT

mixing bowl
knife
measuring cup
measuring spoons
spoon

NOTE: If you double the recipe, do not increase quantity of salt.

1. Core and shred cabbage, cutting into thin strips.
2. Combine all other ingredients in bowl, mixing well.
3. Add cabbage, mixing well enough to coat completely.
4. And you thought this was going to be hard!

ZUCCHINI SALAD

Cold

Serves 2

INGREDIENTS
2 medium-sized zucchini
1/4 cup vegetable oil
4 Tbsp. vinegar (red wine
      vinegar preferable)
1/2 tsp. dill or to taste
1/4 tsp salt or to taste

EQUIPMENT
mixing bowl
measuring cup
measuring spoons
large spoon
grater or large knife
paper towels

1. Rinse zucchini under cool water and paper towel dry.
2. Cut off tips.
3. Coarsely grate or chop into thin strips about 1 inch long.
4. Place zucchini in bowl, add other ingredients and mix well.

APPLE-CELERY SALAD

Cold

INGREDIENTS
1 large "red delicious" apple
1 stalk celery
2 Tbsp. mayonnaise
1/2 tsp. sugar
1/2 tsp. lemon juice

Serves 2

EQUIPMENT
knife
bowl
measuring spoons

1. Wash, core, and chop apple into small pieces.
2. Wash & chop celery into thin slices.
3. In bowl, combine mayonnaise, sugar and lemon juice and mix well.
4. Add apple and celery to bowl and blend with dressing.

CREAMY CUCUMBER SALAD

Cold

INGREDIENTS
1 large cucumber
creamy dill dressing, p. 172

Serves 2

EQUIPMENT
salad bowl
knife
mixing spoon
peeler

1. Peel cucumber and cut into 1/8" thick slices.
2. Prepare Creamy Dill Dressing.
3. Place cucumber in bowl & pour over enough dressing to moisten thoroughly. Mix.
4. Serve cold.

OIL & VINEGAR DRESSING

We suggest doubling this recipe to keep a convenient stock on hand. Just store in a bottle in the refrigerator.

Makes 3/4 cup

INGREDIENTS

1/2 cup vegetable oil
1/4 cup vinegar
1/4 tsp. dill or basil
1 tsp. garlic powder
1. Mix all ingredients thoroughly.

EQUIPMENT

measuring cup
measuring spoons
bowl or storage
container with lid.
mixing spoon

RUSSIAN DRESSING

Makes 3/4 cup

INGREDIENTS

1/2 cup mayonnaise
1/4 cup catsup
1 Tbsp. lemon juice
1 Tbsp. sweet pickle relish
1/2 tsp. garlic powder
1/4 tsp. salt
1/4 tsp. pepper

NOTE: If you double the recipe, do not increase quantity of salt.
1. Mix all ingredients thoroughly.

EQUIPMENT

measuring cup
measuring spoons
bowl or storage
container with lid.
mixing spoon

CREAMY DILL DRESSING

Makes 1/2 cup

INGREDIENTS
1/4 cup vegetable oil
1/4 cup mayonnaise
1 Tbsp. mustard
1 tsp. lemon juice
1/2 tsp. dill
1/4 tsp. sugar
1/4 tsp. salt
1/4 tsp. pepper

EQUIPMENT
measuring cup
measuring spoons
mixing spoon (or wisk)

NOTE: If you double this recipe, do not increase the quantity of salt.

1. Measure 1/4 cup mayonnaise into measuring cup.
2. Pour oil slowly into mayonnaise mixing well as you pour until you reach 1/2 cup measure. You may want to stop every few moments in order to mix in the oil. (The oil and mayonnaise will separate, otherwise.)
3. While continuing to mix, add other ingredients and beat until creamy.

MISCELLANEOUS...

WHAT ARE HOT DOGS DOING HERE?

It's hard to beat hot dogs for a cheap and easy meal. They're a good break from
cooking all week. Just don't buy cheap dogs. Try our cheesy hot dogs for a real treat. Here are some
cooking methods and variations:

Boil: Classic taste.
Immerse hot dogs into boiling water for 5 mins.

Fry: Charcoal taste.
Over medium heat, fry hot dogs, turning frequently. The dogs are done when they are puffy and
the skin is slightly blackened.

Broil: Plumpest hot dog.
Place hot dog under broiler for approx. 7 mins, turning once.

Optional: Slit hot dog lengthwise. Place sliver of any firm cheese in the cut about 30 seconds before
the hot dog is done.

Serve on buns. Add: Catsup, mustard, sweet pickle relish, onion (chopped), mayonnaise.

BARBECUED SPARERIBS

Preheat oven 350°

INGREDIENTS
6 - 8 spareribs
Basic Barbecue sauce, p. 180

Serves 2

EQUIPMENT
baking pan
spoon
paper towels

1. Prepare barbecue sauce.
2. Place spareribs in baking pan, meat side up.
3. Spoon or brush sauce over ribs, coating evenly.
4. Bake 20 mins.
5. Add more sauce, turn ribs and add sauce if there is any meat on the underside.
   Cook 25 mins. more or until no longer pink inside.

BREADED PORK CHOPS

The problem with pork chops is that they have a tendency to dry out. A good way to prevent this is to bread them. The coating helps seal in the juices and keep the chops tender.

Preheat oven 350°

INGREDIENTS
4 pork chops, about
   1/2″ thick
1 egg
2 tsp. water
1/3 cup flour
1/3 cup seasoned
     bread crumbs

Serves 2

EQUIPMENT
baking pan
shallow bowl
2 plates
measuring cup
measuring spoons
paper towels
fork

1. Break egg into bowl and beat slightly while adding water.
2. Pour bread crumbs and flour onto separate plates.
3. Wash pork chops under cool water and dry with paper towels.
4. Dip one chop at a time into the flour, coating both sides. Pat off excess.
5. Dip chop into egg, coating both sides.
6. Dip chop into bread crumbs, coating completely.
7. Place in baking pan and bake 45 mins. or until no longer pink inside. Turn once at about 20 mins.

BROILED PORTERHOUSE STEAK

Oven on Broil

Serves 2

INGREDIENTS

2 porterhouse steaks
salt & pepper to taste
OPTIONAL:
- 1 tsp. lemon juice and
- 1 tsp. garlic powder or
- 1 Tbsp. teriyaki sauce or
- 1 Tbsp. Worcestershire sauce or
- 1 Tbsp. soy sauce

EQUIPMENT

broiling pan
measuring spoons
knife

1. If you wish to add one of the optional ingredients, poke the steaks with the knife to allow the flavor to run inside.
2. Salt & pepper lightly (omit if you chose soy sauce - it's already salty).
3. Place at least 5 inches from broiler flame.
4. Broil 10-20 mins. (depending upon thickness) turning once. You may want to cut into steaks to check for desired doneness.
   NOTE: In schedule for week 8, steak is served with a baked potato. Bake potato (see pg.161) & set aside. In last 5 mins. of broiling steak, return potato to oven to reheat.

GARLIC BREAD

Oven on broil

Serves 2

INGREDIENTS

1/2 loaf French or sourdough
bread (hard crust)
3 Tbsp. butter or margarine
1 tsp. garlic powder

EQUIPMENT

small saucepan
knife
spoon

1. Slice bread horizontally in two even pieces.
   Place crust side down on broiler pan.
2. In saucepan, melt margarine over low heat, stirring in garlic powder as it melts.
3. When margarine is completely melted, spoon evenly over bread.
4. Place bread under broiler for 1 min. or until golden brown on top.
   Watch closely that it doesn't burn.

BASIC BARBECUE SAUCE

Makes 1/2 cup

INGREDIENTS
1/2 cup catsup
1/2 tsp. Worcestershire sauce
1/2 tsp. vinegar
1 Tbsp. sugar
1/4 tsp. salt
1/4 tsp. pepper

EQUIPMENT
small saucepan
mixing bowl
measuring cup
measuring spoons
large spoon

1. Mix all ingredients thoroughly.
2. Cook over low heat for 5 mins., stirring occasionally.

RECIPE INDEX

THE END...

© 1982